16 CUTE TOYS TO CROCHET

Cutest Crochet Creations

ALISON NORTH

Tuva Publishing

www.tuvapublishing.com

Address Merkez Mah. Cavusbasi Cad. No71
Cekmekoy - Istanbul 34782 / Turkey
Tel +9 0216 642 62 62

Cutest Crochet Creations

First Print 2018 / July

All Global Copyrights Belong To
Tuva Tekstil ve Yayıncılık Ltd.

Content Crochet

Editor in Chief Ayhan DEMİRPEHLİVAN

Project Editor Kader DEMİRPEHLİVAN

Designer Alison NORTH

Technical Editors Leyla ARAS, Büşra ESER

Graphic Designers Ömer ALP, Abdullah BAYRAKÇI, Zilal ÖNEL

Photography Tuva Publishing

Crochet Tech Editor Wendi CUSINS

ISBN 978-605-9192-34-7

Contents

INTRODUCTION 7

MATERIALS USED 8

TECHNIQUES

GENERAL INFORMATION FOR MAKING AMIGURUMI 12

ADAPTING THE DESIGN 13

CROCHET TERMINOLOGY 14

CROCHET BASICS 14

SPECIAL STITCHES USED IN AMIGURUMI 17

CROCHET TECHNIQUES FOR AMIGURUMI 19

ASSEMBLING AMIGURUMI PIECES TOGETHER 22

EMBRIODERY STITCHES 26

PROJECTS

SUNNY AND BILL 30

RHIANNON THE BUNNY 36

CYNTHIA DOLL 44

OTIS THE DONKEY 50

NOVA THE GIRAFFE 56

FRANKIE THE BUNNY 62

JAMES THE FOX 68

MEADOW THE COW 74

BORIS THE BEAR 80

LUKA THE LION 86

SCARLETT 92

KOBI THE CROCODILE 100

NUTMEG THE SQUIRREL 106

LUCY LAMB 112

ZACK WHALE AND POPPY NARWHAL 116

MILO THE MONKEY 122

project gallery

Page 30

Page 36

Page 44

Page 50

Page 56

Page 62

Page 68

Page 74

Page 80

Page 86

Page 92

Page 100

Page 106

Page 112

Page 116

Page 122

Introduction

Growing up, watching my mother knit, I remember always wanting to be involved. With her help I made my first knitted bear when I was 10 years old; he was blue, and I named him Winston. My mother loved crafts. She was always making something, and she was a big influence on me and my work.

As the years passed I had children of my own, and with them came a desire to make their toys. I decided to learn to crochet. I bought my first hook, a ball of yarn, and sat poring over YouTube videos for hours on end. At first, I started with beginner videos; watching them and pausing, over and over again, trying to get to grips with simple techniques like holding the crochet hook or making a basic chain. After hours of practice I finally made a basic swatch of double crochet! I was so pleased with myself.

The very next day I went back to the yarn store, bought what I needed, and my obsession with crochet began.

I made so many blankets and baby hats I didn't know what to do with them. I decided to open my Etsy Shop, KornflakeStew, to sell the things I made, and as the business grew so did my confidence.

I was itching to learn new things and that's when I discovered the world of Amigurumi. My Etsy shop became less about blankets and hats and more about creating adorable soft toys, of all different colours and personalities, like the ones in this book.

Writing this book has been a dream come true and I hope you enjoy making my characters as much as I enjoyed creating them.

Alison North

MATERIALS USED

THE YARNS

You can use just about any yarn to crochet with, and through experimenting with different types of materials you will find what suits best for each project you work on.
I mainly use cotton for crocheting toys; it's just a personal preference. I like the way it looks, there are endless colour options, it keeps its shape well, and is also very soft and durable. However, there are some downsides to cotton: as it is made up of lots of strands it can be a little splitty and the hook sometimes doesn't slide as easily but, for me, the result is worth it.

I sometimes use Merino wool, which is incredibly soft and slides on the hook with ease, although I find the colour choice is not as varied as with cotton and it can be expensive.

Acrylic yarns are great for beginners; it comes in many colours and weights and is usually much cheaper. When I first began crocheting I used acrylic yarn. Although I am not so keen on it now (it's less durable than wool and cotton and tends to have a 'bobbling' effect) I still like a lot of acrylic yarns. It's all about personal choice, experimentation, and finding out what you like.

In this book I use a wide range of DMC yarns.

DMC NATURA JUST COTTON

Natura Just Cotton is a yarn made from 100% cotton. It has a matte finish, which makes it lovely to use for crochet. The long fibers give it softness and strength, creating a fabric with good stitch definition.

DMC WOOLLY

Woolly is a light weight yarn made of 100% Merino wool, recognized as the best wool in the world. It is 100% natural and renewable. It is easy to care for (machine-washable) and pleasant to work with.

DMC WOOLLY 5

Woolly 5 is a medium weight yarn with volume and softness. It is also made of 100% machine-washable Merino wool, a natural and renewable fiber.

THE HOOKS

I love using the Clover Amour Hooks which are ergonomic, comfortable and easy to hold. Each size hook has its own color, making it easy to remember which hook you're using.

HOOK SIZE CONVERSION TABLE

It's important to select the right sized crochet hook for your project. A rule of thumb is the thinner the yarn, the smaller the hook you'll need. Using a hook which is too large for the yarn will create unsightly gaps between the stitches.

The size of the crochet hook, the yarn thickness (otherwise known as the yarn's weight) and your tension (I'll go into greater detail about tension in the "techniques" section) will determine the the size of the finished toy: Large crochet hooks, thick yarns and loose tension will create larger toys.

I personally like to use an Aran/worsted weight yarn with a 3mm hook. This generally seen as a small hook to use on such a thick yarn but it's all about personal preference. Try experimenting to find the hook size and yarn combination you are most comfortable with.

Another point to consider when selecting a crochet hook is the material its made of (steel, aluminium, wood, plastic etc.). This won't affect the look of the finished toy in any way, but it will affect how it feels to crochet with. it's just another point of personal preference.

US	U.S.	UK/Canada
-	2.00 mm	14
B-1	2.25 mm	13
C-2	2.75 mm	12
-	3.00 mm	11
D-3	3.25 mm	10
E-4	3.50 mm	-
F-5	3.75 mm	9
G-6	4.00 mm	8
7	4.50 mm	7
H-8	5.00 mm	6
I-9	5.50 mm	5
J-10	6.00 mm	4
K-10 ½	6.50 mm	3

THE STUFFING

When it comes to stuffing your toys, there are quite a few options available. Whichever stuffing you choose, make sure it is fluffy and does not clump. I used **polyester fiberfill** (also known as polyfill or fiberfill) for the stuffing in all the toys.

Polyester pellets (which are heavier than stuffing) can also be used if you want a bit of weight in your toy. You can also combine polyfill with pellets while stuffing.

Please do NOT use stuffing like rice or beans, which might rot and decay, which could attract creepy crawlies.

THE STITCH MARKERS

When making toys in continuous rounds stitch markers are essential, they mark the end of the round so you know where your new round will start, this also helps because if you find you have made a mistake and the stitch count isn't adding up, you will be able to just pull out the row you have just made rather than the whole thing. As you will probably

notice in the pictures for this book I like to use a scrap of yarn as a marker in a contrasting colour (just so you know where it is) I always place it just before the first stitch in a new round and move it up every round. A scrap of yarn has its downsides as a marker as it can easily be pulled out by mistake (which I have done many many times!) but its just what I have got used to. You can buy lots of different types of marker, from plastic markers which are very inexpensive for a big pack to handmade individual markers which can be quite pricey.

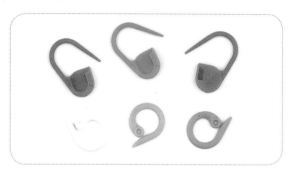

THE YARN (TAPESTRY) NEEDLE

This needle is needed for joining the different crochet pieces together, as well as for weaving in the yarn ends.

Preferably use a blunt-tipped needle which will not split the yarn. You could also use a bent-tip tapestry needle. Make sure the eye of the needle is large enough for the yarn you're using. We also find that the metal needles work much better with amigurumi than the plastic needles.

SAFETY EYES

Safety eyes come in lots of sizes and colours and for this book I use black 11/32" (9 mm) and ¼" (6 mm) eyes. The eye comes in two parts, the front button with a shaft and a plastic washer. I would always recommend buying the best quality eyes as I have had cheap versions in the past which come lose easily. To add an eye to a toy place it through a gap between stitches, you can keep moving them around until you are happy with their position, then from the inside of the toy attach the washer to the shaft and snap into place as far as they will go. I wouldn't recommend using them if you are giving the toy to a child under 3 years old. They do stay in place very well and you probably wouldn't be able to remove them once attached but I would always rather go for embroidery for younger children.

Sometimes it is easy enough to attach these eyes using only your fingers. For those who find it difficult, there is a safety eye insertion tool which can be used to attach the washers.

THE EMBROIDERY FLOSS / PERLE COTTON THREAD

DMC has wide range of Perle or Stranded cottons, which can be used to embellish your toys. You can use them to embroider facial features, or enhance their overall appearance by adding cross-stitch motifs or embroidered flowers.

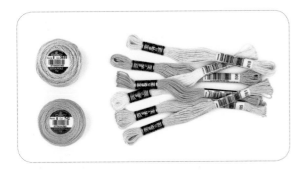

THE SEWING NEEDLE & THREAD

When applying applique (either crocheted pieces or fabric bits), use a good quality needle and thread to sew the pieces on securely.

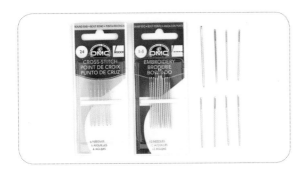

THE OTHER MATERIALS

Small Scissors
Straight Pins (with large heads)
Pompom makers
Buttons

GENERAL INFORMATION FOR MAKING AMIGURUMI

CHOOSING THE HOOK

Use a hook which is a size or two smaller than what is recommended on the yarn label. The fabric created should be tight enough so that the stuffing does not show through the stitches.

RIGHT SIDE VS WRONG SIDE OF THE FABRIC

It is important to be able to distinguish between the 'right' (front) and 'wrong' (back) side of the crocheted fabric.

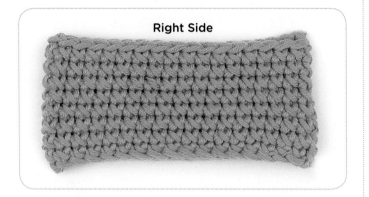

Right Side

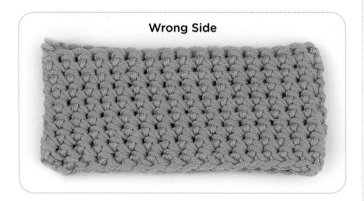

Wrong Side

When working in a spiral or joined round, the right side of the fabric is always facing you. Working in rows or turned rounds, it will alternate between 'right' and 'wrong' side.

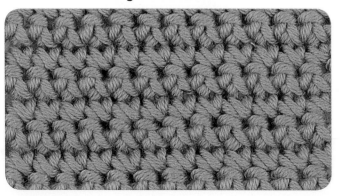

Single Crochet Rows

WORKING IN A SPIRAL

Most of the amigurumi pieces are worked in a continuous spiral to create the dimensional shapes needed. Working in a spiral means that at the end of a round, you do not join (or close) with a slip stitch into the first stitch of the round. When you get to the end of the round, you start the next round by just working a stitch into the next stitch (which is the first stitch of the previous round).

USING STITCH MARKERS

When working in a spiral, it is important to keep track of the round you are working on as well as the stitch count for the round. To do this, use a stitch marker placed in the last stitch of the round. Some people prefer marking the first stitch of the round. Whichever you choose, keep consistent throughout project piece.

Hint Count your stitches after each round (and row) to ensure you have the correct stitch count.

WORKING IN JOINED (CLOSED) ROUNDS

Some parts of an amigurumi pattern might have 'joined rounds'. This is where, at the end of the round, you join with a slip stitch in the first stitch of the round. The next round starts with a number of chain stitches (based on height of the stitches used), and then you continue working stitches for the next round.

Note Do not turn at the end of each joined round, unless instructed to do so.

WORKING IN ROWS

For some accessories or patches for your amigurumi, you will need to work in rows. Each row starts by turning the piece and working some chain stitches (known as the 'turning chain'). The number of chain stitches worked is based on the height of the stitches used.

STUFFING

There are many different types of stuffing such as polyester, wool, cotton, bamboo and even corn stuffing. I use hollowfibre polyester stuffing because its fairly inexpensive, can be easily found in shops and online, is washable and I like the end result. You may think that stuffing seems like the easy part but I find it can be trickier than you'd think. To avoid lumpy looking toys add small amounts at a time but make sure to add as much as you can without stretching the fabric and creating unsightly gaps. If stuffing arms and legs I find it helpful to roll the arm/leg between your hand while adding the stuffing bit by bit. A lot of the time I don't stuff the arms at all so if I don't mention stuffing at the end of a section it's probably because I left it unstuffed.

ADAPTING THE DESIGN

There are many ways you can make your amigurumi toy unique.

Size By choosing a different weight yarn, you can make your toys either bigger (using thicker yarn) or smaller (using thinner yarn or thread). Remember to change your hook size too.

Colors This is the easiest way to make your toy unique. Select colors to match décor or personal preference.

Characteristics Changing the facial features of toys, gives them a whole new character. By adding (or removing) embellishments to the overall toy, can change the whole look of it.

Eyes Just by changing the size or color of the eyes, can create a totally different facial expression. Instead of using safety eyes, you can use buttons or beads for eyes. If there is a safety concern, you can sew on small bits of felt for eyes or embroider the features.

Blusher Adding some color to the cheeks, is another way of changing the character of toys. You can apply cosmetic pink blusher or eyeshadow using a small makeup brush or cotton bud (Q-Tip). Another way to do this, is to rub a red pencil on a piece of fabric, pressing down hard. Then rub the 'red' fabric on the cheeks as blusher.

Applique Patches Whether they are crocheted, fabric or felt (or a combination of these), adding appliqué patches to your doll is a great way to make your toys distinctive. They can be facial features, such as eyes, noses, mouths, cheeks, and maybe even ears. You can also make novelty appliqué patches to use as embellishment on the toys. For example – flowers on a dress, eye-patch for a pirate, overall patch for a farmer. The creativity becomes endless.

Embroidery By adding embroidery stitches to the face, the character of the toy can change. Whether you use plain embroidery stitches (straight stitch, back stitch, etc.) or fancy ones (satin stitch, French knot, bullion stitch, etc.), your toy will take on a personality of its own. You can also use the cross-stitch technique to create a unique look.

Note Embroider all facial features to make a child-safe toy.

Crochet Surface Stitches This technique is worked on a finished crochet fabric. It can be used for outlines, emphasis or decoration.

Pompoms These little balls are very versatile. Making them in different sizes, you can use them as bunny tails, or to decorate the toy. A great tool to use is the Clover pompom maker, which comes in various sizes. You can also make them using other methods, like wrapping around a fork or piece of cardboard.

Adding Accessories To create your one-of-a-kind toy, you can add various decorations to them. Colored buttons can be used in a variety of ways to spice things up. Using small ribbons and bows can feminize dolls. Attaching a small bunch of flowers or small basket to a doll's hand, tells a new story.

However you choose to give your toy character, each one ends up being unique!

CROCHET TERMINOLOGY

This book uses US crochet terminology.

BASIC CONVERSION CHART

US	UK
slip stitch (sl st)	slip stitch (sl st)
chain (ch)	chain (ch)
single crochet (sc)	double crochet (dc)
double crochet (dc)	treble crochet (tr)
half-double crochet (hdc)	half treble (htr)
treble (triple) crochet (tr)	double treble (dtr)

ABBREVIATIONS OF THE BASIC STITCHES

ch	Chain Stitch
sl st	Slip Stitch
sc	Single Crochet Stitch
hdc	Half-Double Crochet Stitch
dc	Double Crochet Stitch
tr	Treble (or Triple) Crochet Stitch

CONCISE ACTION TERMS

dec	Decrease (reduce by one or more stitches)
inc	Increase (add one or more stitches)
join	Join two stitches together, usually with a slip stitch. (Either to complete the end of a round or when introducing a new ball or color of yarn)
rep	Repeat (the previous marked instructions)
turn	Turn your crochet piece so you can work back for the next row/round
yo	Yarn over the hook. (Either to pull up a loop or to draw through the loops on hook)
BLO	Back loops only
FLO	Front loops only

STANDARD SYMBOLS USED IN PATTERNS

[ ]	Work instructions within brackets as many times as directed
( )	Work instructions within parentheses in same stitch or space indicated
*	Repeat the instructions following the single asterisk as directed
**	1) Repeat instructions between asterisks as many times as directed; or 2) Repeat from a given set of instructions

CROCHET BASICS

SLIP KNOT

Almost every crochet project starts with a slip knot on the hook. This is not mentioned in any pattern – it is assumed.

To make a slip knot, form a loop with your yarn (the tail end hanging behind your loop); insert the hook through the loop, and pick up the ball end of the yarn. Draw yarn through loop. Keeping loop on hook, gently tug the tail end to tighten the knot. Tugging the ball end tightens the loop.

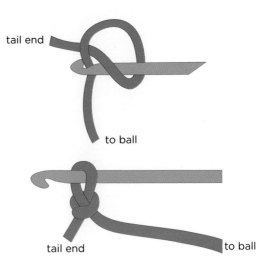

YARN OVER (YO)

This is a common practice, especially with the taller stitches.

With a loop on your hook, wrap the yarn (attached to the ball) from back to front around the shaft of your hook.

CHAIN STITCH (CH)

The chain stitch is the foundation of most crochet projects. The foundation chain is a series of chain stitches in which you work the first row of stitches.

To make a chain stitch, you start with a slip knot (or loop) on the hook. Yarn over and pull the yarn through the loop on your hook (first chain stitch made). For more chain stitches, repeat: Yarn over, pull through loop on hook.

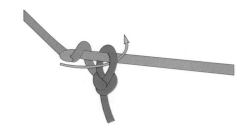

Hint Don't pull the stitches too tight, otherwise they will be difficult to work in.

When counting chain stitches, do not count the slip knot, nor the loop on the hook. Only count the number of 'v's.

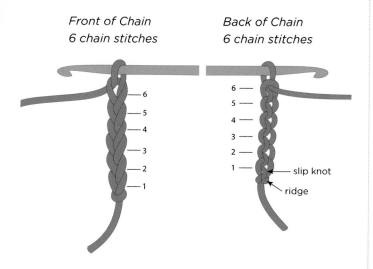

Front of Chain
6 chain stitches

Back of Chain
6 chain stitches

slip knot

ridge

SLIP STITCH (SL ST)

Starting with a loop on your hook, insert hook in stitch or space specified and pull up a loop, pulling it through the loop on your hook as well.

The slip stitch is commonly used to attach new yarn and to join rounds.

Attaching a New Color or New Ball of Yarn (or Joining with a Slip Stitch (join with sl st)).

Make a slip knot with the new color (or yarn) and place loop on hook. Insert hook from front to back in the (usually) first stitch (unless specified otherwise). Yarn over and pull loop through stitch and loop on hook (slip stitch made).

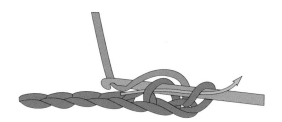

SINGLE CROCHET (SC)

Starting with a loop on your hook, insert hook in stitch or space specified and draw up a loop (two loops on hook). Yarn over and pull yarn through both the loops on your hook (first sc made).

The height of a single crochet stitch is one chain high.

When working single crochet stitches into a foundation chain, begin the first single crochet in the second chain from the hook. The skipped chain stitch provides the height of the stitch.

At the beginning of a single crochet row or round, start by making one chain stitch (to get the height) and work the first single crochet stitch into first stitch (Note: The one chain stitch is never counted as a single crochet stitch).

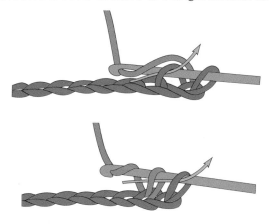

HALF-DOUBLE CROCHET (HDC)

Starting with a loop on your hook, yarn over hook before inserting hook in stitch or space specified and draw up a loop (three loops on hook). Yarn over and pull yarn through all three loops (first hdc made).

The height of a half-double crochet stitch is two chains high.

When working half-double crochet stitches into a foundation chain, begin the first stitch in the third chain from the hook. The two skipped chains provide the height. When starting a row or round with a half-double crochet stitch, make two chain stitches and work in the first stitch (Note: The two chain stitches are never counted as a half-double stitch).

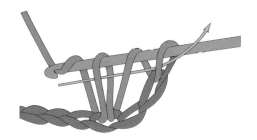

DOUBLE CROCHET (DC)

Starting with a loop on your hook, yarn over hook before inserting hook in stitch or space specified and draw up a loop (three loops on hook). Yarn over and pull yarn through two loops (two loops remain on hook). Yarn over and pull yarn through remaining two loops on hook (first dc made).

The height of a double crochet stitch is three chains high.

When working double crochet stitches into a foundation chain, begin the first stitch in the fourth chain from the hook.

The three skipped chains count as the first double crochet stitch. When starting a row or round with a double crochet stitch, make three chain stitches (which count as the first double crochet), skip the first stitch (under the chains) and work a double crochet in the next (second) stitch. On the following row or round, when you work in the 'made' stitch, you will be working in the top chain (3rd chain stitch of the three chains).

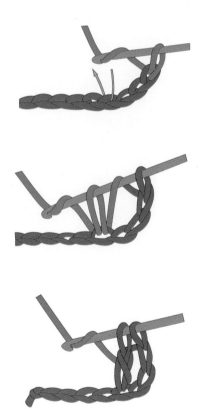

TREBLE (OR TRIPLE) CROCHET (TR)

Starting with a loop on your hook, yarn over hook twice before inserting hook in stitch or space specified and draw up a loop (four loops on hook). Yarn over and pull yarn through two loops (three loops remain on hook). Again, make a yarn over and pull yarn through two loops (two loops remain on hook). Once more, yarn over and pull through remaining two loops (first tr made).

The height of a treble crochet stitch is four chains high. When working treble crochet stitches into a foundation chain, begin the first stitch in the fifth chain from the hook. The four skipped chains count as the first treble crochet stitch. When starting a row or round with a treble crochet stitch, make four chain stitches (which count as the first treble crochet), skip the first stitch (under the chains) and work a treble crochet in the next (second) stitch. On the following row or round, when you work in the 'made' stitch, you will be working in the top chain (4th chain stitch of the four chains).

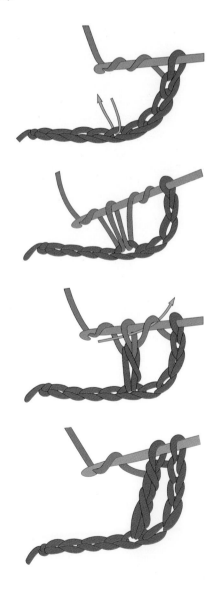

SPECIAL STITCHES USED IN AMIGURUMI

INVISIBLE SINGLE CROCHET DECREASE (INV-DEC)

Insert the hook into the front loops of the next 2 stitches (3 loops on hook).

Yarn over and draw through first two loops on hook (2 loops remain on hook).

Yarn over and draw through both loops on hook (inv-dec made).

Note If you prefer, you can use the normal single crochet decrease stitch.

SINGLE CROCHET INCREASE (INC)

Work 2 single crochet stitches in the same stitch indicated.

SINGLE CROCHET DECREASE - "NORMAL DECREASE" (SC-DEC)

Insert hook in next stitch and pull up a loop, (two loops on hook).

Insert hook in next stitch and pull up a loop (three loops on hook).

Yarn over, draw through all three loops on hook.

Hint Use the invisible decrease (inv-dec) when working in the continuous spiral rounds and use the normal decrease (sc-dec) when working in rows.

PICOT STITCH

The picot stitch is mainly used as a decorative stitch for edging blankets etc in this book I use it as a shaping stitch to create a point on leaves.

Chain 3, insert your hook back into the top of the stitch you are working from, yarn over and pull through all loops.

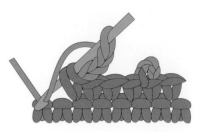

CROCHET TECHNIQUES FOR AMIGURUMI

BACK RIDGE OF FOUNDATION CHAIN

The back ridge (also called back bumps or back bars) is found on wrong side of the foundation chain. It consists of single loops behind the 'v-loops'. To work in the back ridge, one inserts the hook from front to back through the back ridge loop to pull up the yarn. Working in the Back Ridge gives a neater finish to projects.

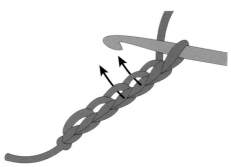

CHANGING COLORS / ATTACHING NEW YARN

With the current color, work the last stitch before the color change up to the last step of the stitch. Using the new color, yarn over hook, pull new color through remaining loops on hook.

New color / yarn

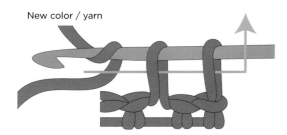

CLOSE THE OPENING

Working in the stitches of the last round, insert the yarn needle from back to front through the front loop of each stitch around. Gently pull the yarn to tighten the hole. Once the opening is closed, secure the yarn. Insert the needle back through the center of the ring and taking care (squashing the stuffing), bring it out at an inconspicuous place on the piece. Work a few weaving stitches before inserting the needle back through the stuffed piece and out at another point. Cut the yarn close to the piece so that it retracts into the stuffing.

CROCHETING AROUND A FOUNDATION CHAIN

When you want to start an oval piece rather than a round piece, I use this a lot for making ears but also sometimes for starting a main part of a character.

Start with the required amount of stitches in a chain. Single crochet into the second chain from the hook (if making

an oval this will usually also be an increase stitch) and in each chain along. The last chain is where you need to put your increases (this will be indicated on the pattern) as you make the increases you will naturally turn to work up the other side of the foundation chain (this will be the other loop of the foundation chain).

FASTEN OFF

After the last single crochet stitch is worked, work a slip stitch in the next stitch. Cut the yarn, leaving a tail. With the tail, yarn over and pull the tail through the stitch.

FITTING SAFETY EYES

Choose and mark the positions for the eyes (or nose) on the front of the face. Insert the shank of the eye (or nose) through the fabric from right side to wrong side. (The eye is on the front side, the shank sticks out at the back.) Attach the locking washer onto the shank and push down firmly to lock it tightly. You can use a safety eye insertion tool for doing this.

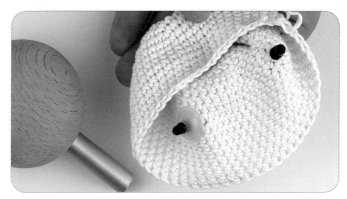

FRONT AND BACK LOOPS

Every stitch has what looks like 'v's on the top. There are two loops that make up the 'v'. The front loop is the loop closest to you and the back loop is the loop furthest from you. Generally, we work in both loops – under both the front and back loops. Working in either the front or back loops only, creates a decorative ridge (made up of the unworked loops).

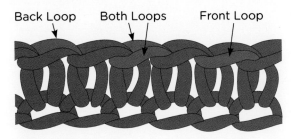

Back Loop   Both Loops   Front Loop

Note Work all stitches under both loops unless otherwise instructed.

INVISIBLE JOIN

After the last stitch is worked (do not slip stitch in next stitch), cut the yarn leaving a tail and pull the tail through the last stitch. Using the tail and a yarn needle, skip the next stitch and insert the needle under both loops of the following stitch. Then insert the needle into the back loop of the last stitch made (the same stitch where the tail came through) and also through the horizontal loop of the stitch (for stability). Gently tug the yarn so that it looks like a "stitch" and matches the others. Secure this "stitch" and weave in the tail.

JOIN WITH SC (SINGLE CROCHET STANDING STITCH)

With a slip knot on hook, insert hook into stitch or space specified and pull up a loop (two loops on hook). Yarn over and pull through both loops on hook (first single crochet made).

JOIN WITH SLIP KNOT

Using the yarn, make a slip knot. Do not insert your hook through loop. Insert your hook in the stitch or space indicated and place the loop of the slip knot on the loop. Gently pull the loop through the stitch, keeping the knot at the back. Continue with the pattern.

WEAVING IN YARN TAILS

Thread the tail onto a yarn needle. Starting close to where the tail begins, preferably working on the wrong side, weave the tail through the back of stitches (preferably of the same color) to hide the yarn. When done, trim the tail close to the fabric.

For weaving in ends on an already stuffed pieces, you can secure the yarn close to the piece and then insert the needle through the stuffing and out the other side. If you want, you can do this a few times. When done, cut the yarn close to the toy and let the end disappear inside.

MAGIC RING (OR ADJUSTABLE RING)

1 Form a loop with the yarn, keeping the tail end of the yarn behind the working yarn (the yarn attached to the ball).

2 Insert the hook through the loop (from front to back), and pull the working yarn through the loop (from back to front). Do not tighten up the loop.

3 Using the working yarn, make a chain stitch (to secure the ring). This chain stitch does NOT count as first stitch.

4 Work the required stitches into the ring (over the tail strand). When all the stitches are done, gently tug the tail end to close the ring, before joining the round (if specified). Remember, make sure this tail is firmly secured before weaving in the end.

Note If you prefer, you can use any type of "ring" to start your project (or start with ch-2, and working the first round in the second chain from hook). The advantage of using the adjustable Magic Ring, is that when it is tightened, it closes the hole completely.

Tip Secure your Magic Ring after the first few rounds and before you start stuffing.

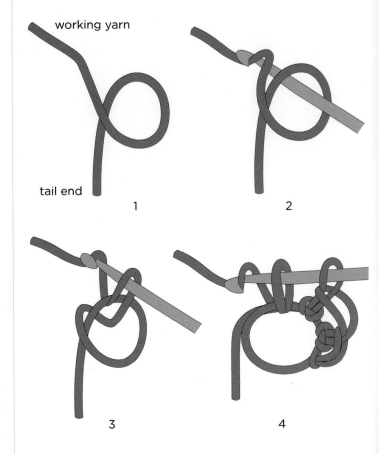

working yarn

tail end

1   2

3   4

ASSEMBLING AMIGURUMI PIECES TOGETHER

Sewing all the amigurumi pieces together can sometimes be a daunting task. Have no fear! There are lots of resources available on the internet showing you how it can be done.

WAYS OF JOINING

FASTENING OFF A CLOSED PIECE

When you are finished the piece you are working on you will usually have 6 stitches left and a small hole that you will need to close neatly. Cut the yarn leaving a long tail. Thread the end onto your tapestry needle, insert the needle from the centre and put it under the front loop of the first stitch, weave in and out of the front loops of the remaining 5 stitches. Pull the tail and the hole will tighten and disappear.

Make a double knot under any stitch nearby to secure the end then take the tail through the finished piece (this will also hide the knot inside the work) pull the tail and cut, this will hide the tail inside the finished piece.

FINISHING AND CLOSING OPEN PIECES

I mainly use this technique when closing arms, legs, ears etc as it helps to make the arm/leg lay flat against the finished piece.

If necessary, stuff the piece you are working on before finishing. Flatten the top of the piece with your fingers and crochet through both sets of stitches to crochet it closed, you should end up with half the number of stitches that were left in the round. Leave a long tail for sewing. Where possible always keep a long yarn tail for sewing the piece in place unless stated that you can finish off and cut the yarn.

ATTACHING PIECES (SEWING TOGETHER)

This is probably the part that most people like the least! To make life easier I find it definitely helps to pin the parts in place first as I have spent far too long un-doing limbs that are wonky in my time as a crocheter, It can be very frustrating. Always use the long tail you left when finishing pieces to sew parts together.

Sewing an open piece to a closed piece (usually sewing a head to a neck) Start by pinning the head in place and threading your tail end onto your tapestry needle. I like to start at the back of the head. Put the needle under a stitch on the head following the natural curve of the neck. Then thread the tail back under the next stitch on the neck, when you go back into the head for the next stitch put it back into the same place where the last stitch came from and bring it out a stitch along, continue working stitches all around the neck and head until it is closed.

ATTACHING FLAT PIECES

To add crocheted cheeks or spots to the finished piece, always use the tail of yarn used to crochet the piece. When you made the cheek /spot you will have a beginning tail as well as an end tail. Keep this tail as well. Thread your tapestry with the beginning tail first, place the cheek on the face and use your needle to take the beginning tail through the head. This will keep the cheek in place while you use the other tail to sew around the edge. When you have sewn all around the edge of the cheek take the yarn tail through the head to the same spot where the other tail is hanging out, using both tail ends tie a double knot then hide both tails inside the head. Use this same method to add spots.

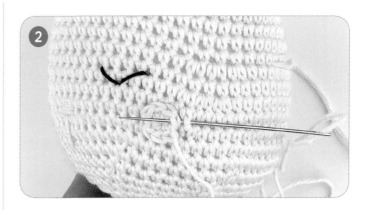

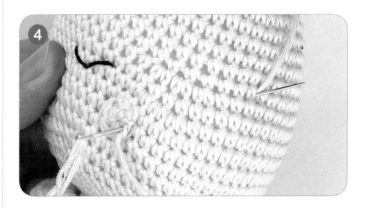

SEWING ARMS AND LEGS

Start by pinning the arm/leg in place. Thread your tapestry needle with the yarn end of the arm/leg Sew under a stitch on the body and then back under the next stitch along on the arm, continue along into the body then into the arm/leg until you get to the end. To secure take the end inside the body and bring it out under a stitch underneath the arm/leg Make a double knot then hide the tail inside the body.

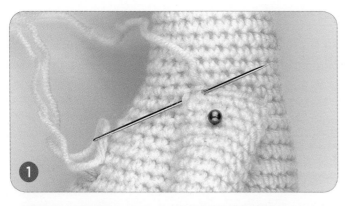

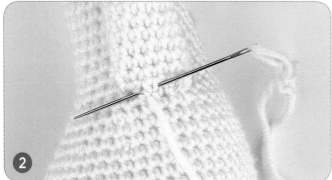

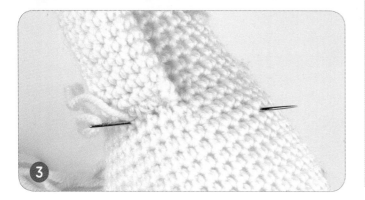

GAUGE

Gauge is how tight or loose you hold your yarn when crocheting. This is very important when crocheting garments so that they will fit a particular size but not as important when making toys. You want to try and achieve neat consistent stitches not necessarily tight stitches, you don't want your hands to ache and you don't want it to feel uncomfortable to crochet. Your tension, hook size and yarn weight will all effect the size of the finished toy. Your tension can also be influenced by the way you are sitting and even your mood, for example if you are feeling a little stressed your stitches may be tighter than usual, for this reason I would recommend crocheting both arms/legs/ears in the same sitting, so you will get them both the same size. The only thing you really want is for there to not be any gaps between stitches so that the stuffing doesn't show through, experiment with hook sizes and yarn weights and practice, practice, practice! As an example, the photo below shows the difference in my tension on different days, I used the same yarn and the same hook size.

SKILL LEVEL SYMBOLS AND DECSCRIPTION

✱	Easy	Project uses basic stitches, repetitive stitch patterns, simple color changes, and simple shaping and finishing
✱✱	Intermediate	Project uses a variety of more advanced techniques, including color patterns, mid-level shaping and finishing
✱✱✱	Challenging	Project has stitch patterns, techniques and dimension, such as non-repeating patterns, multi-color techniques, detailed shaping and refined finishing

WAYS OF SEWING JOINS

There are many different sewing stitches you can use to join pieces together. Everyone develops their own preferences. Practice the various sewing stitch techniques and see which ones you like and which one(s) gives you the nicest finish.

As mentioned, the internet is a great help to identify the "right" sewing stitch for the job and has many tutorials for them. However, the basic stitches used are the Whipstitch and Mattress Stitch (or variation thereof).

WHIPSTITCH

This stitch is commonly used to join "open" to "open" pieces. With both pieces right-side facing, insert your needle through a crocheted stitch on the first piece, from front to back.

Step 1 Bring the needle up through the corresponding stitch on the second piece, from back to front.

Step 2 Insert your needle in the next stitch on the first piece from front to back. Repeat Steps 1 & 2.

MATTRESS STITCH

This is a very versatile stitch and can be virtually "invisible" when tugged gently. It can be used for joining most of the types of pieces together.

Both pieces should be right-side facing. Starting on the first piece, insert your needle under a crocheted stitch, from front to back to front.

On the corresponding stitch on the second piece, insert the needle from front to back to front under the stitch.

Step 1 On the first piece, insert your needle in the same place where it came out and bring it up under the next stitch.

Step 2 On the second piece, insert your needle in the same place where it came out and bring it up under the next stitch. Repeat steps 1 & 2.

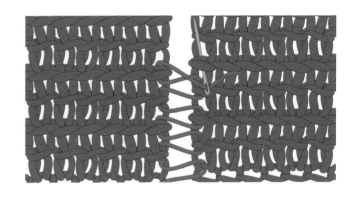

GENERAL TIPS WHEN STITCHING PIECES TOGETHER

1 Make sure both pieces you are sewing together are either right-side facing or wrong-side facing (whichever the pattern call for), unless otherwise instructed.

2 When attaching the Head or Limbs to the Body, make sure they are facing the correct way (unless the pattern says differently). For example, the feet on the Legs should usually point to the front of the body.

3 Use straight pins, stuck straight down into a stuffed piece, to position pieces before sewing.

Hint Try placing and pinning the pieces in different positions to give your toy a different 'look'. Once you're happy with the position, you can then sew the pieces together.

4 Where possible, use the same color yarn of at least one of the pieces getting sewn together.

5 When you need to use a separate strand of yarn for sewing the pieces together (not a yarn tail from either piece), start by leaving a long tail for sewing in later. You can tug this tail gently as you go to keep your stitches neat. When you've finished sewing the joins, go back and secure and weave in the front tail.

Hint By doing it this way, it is easier to pull out and fix things if you make a mistake, than trying to unpick a secured starting point.

EMBRIODERY STITCHES

When embroidering on crochet, it is recommended to insert the needle through the yarn of the stitch and not through the 'holes' between the stitches. This makes it easier to control the placement of the embroidery thread.

BACK STITCH

Bring threaded needle up from wrong to right side of fabric (#1). Insert needle back down a bit before (#2) and bring it out a bit ahead (#3) on the desired outline. Insert the needle back down through the same hole (#1) and bring it out a bit ahead again. Repeat along the desired outline.

BULLION STITCH

Bring threaded needle up from wrong to right side of fabric at the position where you want the knot to start (#1). Insert the needle back into the fabric at the position where you want the knot to end (#2) and back up through the starting point (#1) – without pulling the needle through. Wrap the yarn/thread around tip of needle as many times as needed. Hold the wrapped loops as you gently pull the needle through the fabric and loops to form the Knot. Insert the needle back through the fabric to the wrong side.

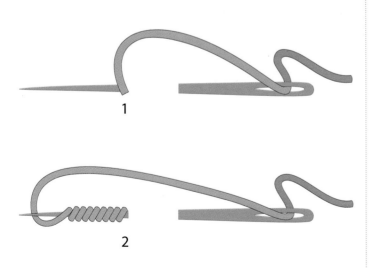

Note To form a Bullion Knot with a slight curve, make more wraps around the tip of the needle than are needed.

FRENCH KNOT

Bring threaded needle up from wrong to right side of fabric at the position where you want the knot (#1). Wrap the yarn/thread twice around needle. Insert the needle back through the fabric, close to where it came up (almost in the same hole as #1). Gently pull the needle and yarn/thread through the wrapped loops to form the knot.

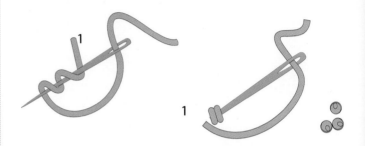

SATIN STITCH

Bring threaded needle up from wrong to right side of fabric (#1). Insert needle along desired outline (#2) and bring it out close to #1. Insert it back, close to #2 and out close to previous stitch. Repeat making stitches close to each other following the desired shape. Take care to make even stitches that are not too tight, so that the fabric still lies flat.

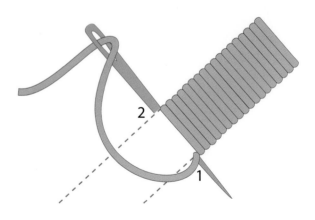

STRAIGHT STITCH

Bring threaded needle up from wrong to right side of fabric at the position you want to start the stitch. Insert the needle back into the fabric at the position you want to end the stitch. Repeat for the remaining stitches.

EMBROIDERY (SLEEPY EYES AND FACIAL FEATURES)

I know very little about embroidery, but you will only need to make basic stitches to make sleepy eyes for your crochet toys. You can use a thin yarn or embroidery floss in black or dark grey.

First of all, to find the centre of the head take a length of yarn, wrap it from the top centre point on the head to the bottom centre point, find the row where the eyes will be placed (according to the pattern) and place a pin at the centre.

Insert your needle and bring it out 4 stitches along on the same row (taking into account the amount of stitches to leave between the eyes). Keep a tail of yarn/thread hanging out and hold it in place, insert the needle back into the starting position and bring it out on the row below and in the middle of the eye.

You then need to put the end of your needle behind the main eye stitch and pull it down as you put the needle back into the head, this will create the middle eyelash and also curve the eye. Bring the needle out at the starting point.

If you just want to leave the eye curved without lashes you can now make a double knot using the beginning tail and hide the tails inside the head. If you'd like to add the sleepy

effect just add another little stitch to each end of the eye before making the double knot and hiding the tails. Make the other eye in the same way.

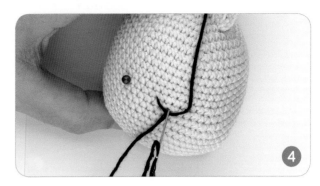

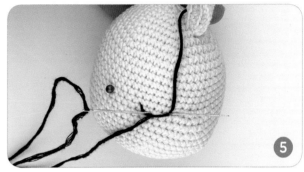

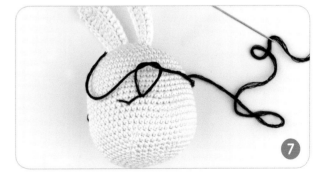

Projects

Sunny and Bill

THESE TWO LOVE BIRDS HAVE HAD A BUSY DAY –
FEASTING ON CAKE CRUMBS AND SINGING AT THE TOP OF
THEIR VOICES. THEY ARE NOW EXHAUSTED AND TAKING A
QUICK NAP

finished size

About 4″ (10 cm) tall; 8″ (20 cm) circumference.

materials

» **DMC Natura Just Cotton**
  » **Main Color (MC)** Ivory (#02) – ¾ oz (25 g); 85 yd (77.5 m)
  » **Color A** Rose Layette (#06) or Turquoise (#49)
    - Small amount for Stripe and Tail Feathers
  » **Color B** Giroflee (#85) or Sable (#03) - Small amount for Beak
  » **Color C** Bougainvillea (#93) or Giroflee (#85) - Small amount for Wings
  » **Flower Colors** Small amounts of Bougainvillea (#93), Ble (#83) & Glicine (#30)
  » **Leaf Colors** Small amounts of Pistache (#13) & Light Green (#12)

» Size C-2 (2.75 mm) Crochet Hook - or size suitable for yarn used.

» Black or Dark Grey Embroidery Floss (or Yarn) – for Eyes
» Toy Stuffing

» **Note** Use Main Hook throughout, unless otherwise stated.

ROUND 1 (Right Side) Starting at the top of the Head, using MC, make a Magic Ring *(see Techniques)*; ch 1, 6 sc in ring; DO NOT JOIN. (6 sc) Tug tail to tighten ring. Mark last stitch.

ROUND 2 [2 sc in next st] around. (12 sc) Move marker each round.

ROUND 3 [Sc in next st, inc *(see Special Stitches)* in next st] around. (18 sc)

ROUND 4 [Sc in each of next 2 sts, inc in next st] around. (24 sc)

ROUND 5 [Sc in each of next 3 sts, inc in next st] around. (30 sc)

ROUND 6 [Sc in each of next 4 sts, inc in next st] around. (36 sc)

ROUND 7 [Sc in each of next 5 sts, inc in next st] around. (42 sc)

ROUND 8 [Sc in each of next 6 sts, inc in next st] around. (48 sc)

ROUNDS 9-25 Sc in each st around. (48 sc)

ROUND 26 Working this round in BLO *(see Techniques)*, [sc in each of next 6 sts, sc-dec *(see Special Stitches)*] around. (42 sc)

ROUND 27 Working in both loops, [sc in each of next 5 sts, sc-dec] around. (36 sc)

Start stuffing Bird firmly to maintain shape, adding more as you go.

ROUND 28 [Sc in each of next 4 sts, sc-dec] around. (30 sc)

ROUND 29 [Sc in each of next 3 sts, sc-dec] around. (24 sc)

ROUND 30 [Sc in each of next 2 sts, sc-dec] around. (18 sc)

ROUND 31 [Sc in next st, sc-dec] around. (12 sc)

ROUND 32 [Sc-dec] around. (6 sc) Finish stuffing the Bird. Fasten off and close *(see Techniques)*.

ROUND 1 (Step 1) (Right Side) Using Color A, ch 35, sc in 2nd ch from hook, sc in each of next 5 ch, hdc in each of next 6 ch, dc in each of next 16 ch, tr in each of next 5 ch, (tr, ch 4, sl st) in last ch.

Step 2 Ch 4, working in unused lps on other side of starting ch, tr in first ch, tr in each of next 5 ch, dc in each of next 16 ch, hdc in each of next 6 ch, sc in each of next 5 ch, 3 sc in last ch; join with sl st to first sc. Finish off leaving a long tail for sewing.

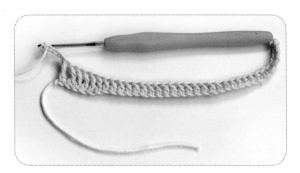

End of Step 1, before the last slip stitch.

Beginning of Step 2.

Feather (Make 2)

ROUND 1 (Right Side) Starting at the tip of Feather, using Color A, make a Magic Ring; ch 1, 6 sc in ring; DO NOT JOIN. (6 sc) Tug tail to tighten ring. Mark last stitch.

ROUND 2 Sc in each st around. (6 sc) Move marker each round.

ROUND 3 [Sc in next st, inc in next st] around. (9 sc)

ROUNDS 4-6 Sc in each st around. (9 sc)

At the end of Round 6, for the first Feather, finish off. For the second Feather, DO NOT FINISH OFF.

Working in first Feather, sc in first st. Move marker to this st.

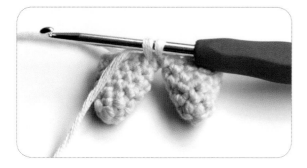

Joining the second Feather to the first Feather.

ROUND 7 Working in first Feather, [sc in next st] around, working in second Feather, sc in each st around to marker. (18 sc)

Working around the joined Feathers.

ROUNDS 8-9 Sc in each st around. (18 sc)

ROW 10 Sc in each of next 13 sts. Leave rem sts unworked. The last stitch should be at the edge of the flattened Tail. If extra (or less) sts are needed to reach the edge, adjust accordingly.

Working across to edge of Tail.

LAST ROW Working through both thicknesses of the flattened Tail, sc in each st across (to close). (9 sc) Finish off leaving a long tail for sewing.

Working across flattened last round to close Tail.

BEAK   •

ROUND 1 (Right Side) Starting at the tip of Beak, using Color B, make a Magic Ring; ch 1, 5 sc in ring; DO NOT JOIN. (5 sc) Tug tail to tighten ring. Mark last stitch.

ROUND 2 Sc in each st around. (5 sc) Move marker each round.

ROUND 3 [Sc in next st, inc in next st] twice, sc in last st. (7 sc) Sl st in next st. Finish off leaving a long tail for sewing.

WINGS (Make 2)   •

ROUND 1 (Right Side) Using Color C, make a Magic Ring; ch 1, (3 sc, 3 hdc, 3 dc, 2 tr, picot, 2 tr, 3 dc, 3 hdc, 3 sc) in ring; join with sl st to first sc. (22 sts) Tug tail to tighten ring. Finish off leaving a long tail for sewing.

Stitches of Wing worked in ring, before joining.

Stripe - With right side of Stripe facing, pin it to the Bird, placing with the widest part of the Stripe at the base of the Bird (the BLO round) and wrapping the narrow part over the top of the head and a little way down the front. Using long tail and yarn needle, sew around the whole Stripe in keep it in place.

Pinning the Stripe over Head

Sewing Stripe in place.

Tail Feathers - Using the long tail and yarn needle, position the Tail Feathers at the base of the Bird to meet up with the wide part of the Stripe and sew in place.

Sewing Tail Feathers in position.

Beak - Using the long tail and yarn needle, position the Beak at the narrow end of the Stripe and sew in place.

Sewing on Beak at end of Stripe.

Wings - Using the tails and yarn needle, position the Wings on either side of the Bird (points of Wings facing towards back of Bird) and sew in place.

Sewing Wings in position.

Eyes - Using the Embroidery Floss (or black yarn), embroider Sleepy Eyes *(see Embroidery Stitches)*, skipping about 3 stitches on either side of Beak.

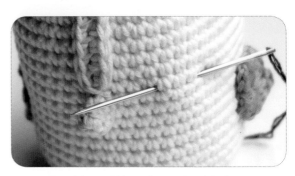

Position of Eyes for embroidering.

Rhiannon the Bunny

RHIANNON IS A FREE-SPIRIT WHO EMBRACES LIFE. SHE
HAS A KIND HEART AND WILL DO ANYTHING FOR HER
LOVED ONES

finished size

About 10½" (27 cm) tall.

materials

» **DMC Natura Just Cotton**
  » **Main Color (MC)** Natural (#03) – 1½ oz (50 g); 170 yd (155 m)
  » **Color A** Ble (#83) – 1½ oz (50 g); 170 yd (155 m) for Dress
  » **Color B** Rose Layette (#06) – small amount for Inner Ears, Cheeks & Collar
  » **Color C** Light Green (#12) – small amount for Headband
  » **Flower Colors** Small amounts of Bougainvillea (#93), Ble (#83) & Glicine (#30)
  » **Leaf Colors** Small amounts of Pistache (#13) & Light Green (#12)

» Size C-2 (2.75 mm) Crochet Hook - or size suitable for yarn used. (Main Hook)
» Size B-1 (2.25 mm) Crochet Hook – for Inner Ears
» Size D-3 (3.25 mm) Crochet Hook - for Dress

» Black or Dark Grey Embroidery Floss (or Yarn) – for Eyes
» Toy Stuffing

» **Note** Use Main Hook throughout, unless otherwise stated.

HEAD

ROUND 1 (Right Side) Starting at the top of the Head, using MC, make a Magic Ring (*see Techniques*); ch 1, 6 sc in ring; DO NOT JOIN. (6 sc) Tug tail to tighten ring. Mark last stitch.

ROUND 2 [2 sc in next st] around. (12 sc) Move marker each round.

ROUND 3 [Sc in next st, inc (*see Special Stitches*) in next st] around. (18 sc)

ROUND 4 [Sc in each of next 2 sts, inc in next st] around. (24 sc)

ROUND 5 [Sc in each of next 3 sts, inc in next st] around. (30 sc)

ROUND 6 [Sc in each of next 4 sts, inc in next st] around. (36 sc)

ROUND 7 [Sc in each of next 5 sts, inc in next st] around. (42 sc)

ROUND 8 [Sc in each of next 6 sts, inc in next st] around. (48 sc)

ROUNDS 9-14 Sc in each st around. (48 sc)

ROUND 15 Sc in each of next 11 sts, [inc in next st] 3 times, sc in each of next 20 sts, [inc in next st] 3 times, sc in each of next 11 sts. (54 sc)

ROUND 16 Sc in each st around. (48 sc)

ROUND 17 Sc in each of next 13 sts, [inc in next st] 3 times, sc in each of next 22 sts, [inc in next st] 3 times, sc in each of next 13 sts. (60 sc)

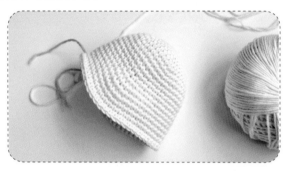

Head - showing shaping of Cheeks.

ROUNDS 18-21 Sc in each st around. (60 sc)

ROUND 22 [Sc in each of next 8 sts, sc-dec (*see Special Stitches*)] around. (54 sc)

ROUND 23 [Sc in each of next 7 sts,] around. (48 sc)

ROUND 24 [Sc in each of next 6 sts, sc-dec] around. (42 sc)

ROUND 25 [Sc in each of next 5 sts, sc-dec] around. (36 sc)

ROUND 26 [Sc in each of next 4 sts, sc-dec] around. (30 sc)

Start stuffing Head firmly (making sure to shape the cheek pouches), adding more as you go.

ROUND 27 [Sc in each of next 3 sts, sc-dec] around. (24 sc)

ROUND 28 [Sc in each of next 2 sts, sc-dec] around. (18 sc)

ROUND 29 [Sc in next st, sc-dec] around. (12 sc)

ROUND 30 [Sc-dec] around. (6 sc) Finish stuffing the Head. Fasten off and close (*see Techniques*).

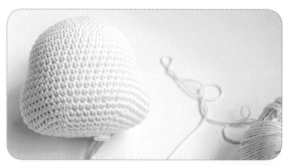

Finished stuffed Head.

CHEEKS (Make 2)

ROUND 1 (Right Side) Using Color B, make a Magic Ring; ch 1, 8 sc in ring; join with sl st to first sc. (8 sc) Tug tail to tighten ring. Finish off leaving a long tail for sewing.

EARS

Inner Ear (Make 2)

ROW 1 (Right Side) Using smaller hook and Color B, ch 11, sc in 2nd ch from hook, sc in each of next 2 ch, hdc in each of next 3 ch, dc in each of next 3 ch, 4 dc in last ch; working in unused lps on other side of starting ch, dc in each of next 3 ch, hdc in each of next 3 ch, sc in each of next 3 ch. (22 sts) Finish off.

Outer Ear (Make 2)

ROW 1 (Wrong Side) Using Main Hook and MC, repeat Row 1 of Inner Ear, but DO NOT FASTEN OFF. (22 sts)

Ear Assembly Holding an Inner and Outer Ear with wrong sides together, with Outer Ear facing, ch 1, working through both thicknesses using back loops of Outer Ear and front loops of Inner Ear, matching stitches and shaping, sc in each st across. (22 sc) Finish off leaving a long tail for sewing.

Repeat for other Ear.

Assembled Ears

HEAD ASSEMBLY – Use photos as guide

Ears - Holding the Head with stuffed cheek pouches on either side, position and sew the Ears to either side at the top of the Head, between Rounds 4 and 8.

Eyes - Using the Floss, embroider Sleepy Eyes *(see Embroidery Stitches)* between Round 16 & 17, about 8 stitches between them.

Nose - Using Color B, embroider Nose using Straight Stitches *(see Embroidery Stitches)* to center front of face, about 4 rounds below the Eyes. Make a few horizontal stitches, and one straight vertical stitch.

Cheeks - Using long tails and yarn needle, position Cheeks on either side of face and sew in place

LEGS (Make 2)

ROUND 1 (Right Side) Using MC, make a Magic Ring; ch 1, 6 sc in ring; DO NOT JOIN. (6 sc) Tug tail to tighten ring. Mark last stitch.

ROUND 2 [2 sc in next st] around. (12 sc) Move marker each round.

ROUND 3 [Sc in next st, inc in next st] around. (18 sc)

ROUNDS 4-18 Sc in each st around. (18 sc)

At the end of the Round 18 - for the First Leg, finish off. For the Second Leg, DO NOT FINISH OFF.

BODY

ROUND 19 (Joining Legs) Ch 3, working on First Leg, sc in last st made, sc in each of next 17 sts; working in ch-sts, sc in each of next 3 ch; working on Second Leg, sc in each of next 18 sts, working in unused lps on other side of ch-3, sc in each of next 3 ch. (42 sc) Move marker to last st made.

ROUNDS 20-30 Sc in each st around. (42 sc)

ROUND 31 [Sc in each of next 5 sts, sc-dec] around. (36 sc)

ROUNDS 32-33 Sc in each st around. (36 sc)

ROUND 34 [Sc in each of next 4 sts, sc-dec] around. (30 sc)

ROUNDS 35-36 Sc in each st around. (30 sc)

Start stuffing Legs and Body firmly, adding more as you go.

Stuffing Legs and Body

ROUND 37 [Sc in each of next 3 sts, sc-dec] around. (24 sc)

ROUNDS 38-40 Sc in each st around. (24 sc)

At the end of Round 40, slip stitch in next st to finish off, leaving a long tail for sewing. Set Body aside.

DRESS

ROUND 1 (Right Side) Starting at the top (neck of Dress), using Color A and larger hook, ch 22, taking care not to twist chain, sc in first ch made to form a ring, sc in each of next 21 ch. (22 sc) Mark last st.

Note Place another marker opposite the first sc in the unused loop of the chain stitch to identify center back of Dress. Do not move this marker.

Continue working in a spiral.

ROUND 2 Inc in next st, sc in each of next 21 sts, inc in last st. (24 sc) Move marker each round.

ROUND 3 Sc in each of next 6 sts, inc in next st, sc in each of next 10 sts, inc in next st, sc in each of next 6 sts. (26 sc)

ROUND 4 Inc in next st, sc in each of next 5 sts, inc in next st, sc in each of next 12 sts, inc in next st, sc in each of next 5 sts, inc in last st. (30 sc)

ROUND 5 [Sc in each of next 4 sts, inc in next st] around. (36 sc)

ROUND 6 [Sc in each of next 5 sts, inc in next st] around. (42 sc)

ROUND 7 Sc in each st around. (42 sc)

ROUND 8 [Sc in each of next 6 sts, inc in next st] around. (48 sc)

ROUND 9 Sc in each st around. (48 sc)

ROUND 10 [Sc in each of next 7 sts, inc in next st] around. (54 sc)

ROUND 11 Sc in each st around. (54 sc)

ROUND 12 Ch 1, dc in each st around. (54 dc)

ROUND 13 Skip ch-1, dc in each st around. (54 dc)

ROUND 14 (Border) [Skip next 2 sts, (sc, 2 dc, sc) in next st] around. (18 shells) Sl st in next st to finish off. Weave in ends.

COLLAR

ROUND 1 With wrong side of Dress's neck facing *(see photo)*, working in unused lps on other side of starting ch, join Color B with sl st to marked ch (center back), ch 3 (counts as first dc), dc in same st as joining, [2 dc in next ch] around; join with sl st to first dc (3rd ch of beg ch-3). (44 dc) Finish off and weave in all ends.

Collar worked with wrong side of Dress facing.

ARMS (Make 2)

ROUND 1 (Right Side) Using MC, make a Magic Ring; ch 1, 8 sc in ring; DO NOT JOIN. (8 sc) Tug tail to tighten ring. Mark last stitch.

ROUNDS 2-12 Sc in each st around. (8 sc) Move marker each round.

At the end of Round 12, change to Color A. Finish off MC.

ROUNDS 13-20 Sc in each st around. (8 sc)

LAST ROW Flatten the last round and working through both thicknesses, sc in each of next 4 sc. Finish off leaving a long tail for sewing.

Sleeve Cuff

ROUND 1 Working in Round 12 of Arm, using Color B, join with sc *(see photos)* around post of any st, [sc in next st] around; join with sl st to first sc. Finish off and weave in all ends.

Repeat for second Arm.

Joining with Single Crochet around Post of Stitches

With slip knot on hook, insert hook around post of any stitch. Yarn over and pull up a loop (2 loops of hook). Yarn over and draw through both loops on hook. (First sc made.)

Working single crochet stitches around Arm.

1. Fold down the Collar and slip Dress onto Body, with the join of Collar at center back.

Dress placed on Body.

2. Using the long tail of Body and yarn needle, position and sew the Head to the Body.

Attaching the Head.

3. Position the Arms on either side of the Dress/Body. Using long tails and yarn needle, sew them in place, working through the Dress into the Body, to secure them. (This also helps to keep the Dress in place.)

Attaching the Arms

ROW 1 Using Color C, ch 41, sc in 2nd ch from hook, [sc in next ch] across. (40 sc)

ROW 2 Ch 1, turn, sc in each st across. (40 sc) Sl st in same st as last sc, ch 40 (First Tie made). Finish off, pulling last st very tight to secure. Weave in ends.

Second Tie
Working on other side of Headband, join with sl st between the two rows; ch 40. Finish off, pulling last st very tight to secure. Weave in all ends.

Flower (Make 9 – 3 in each Flower Color)

ROUND 1 (Right Side) Make a Magic Ring; [ch 6, sl st in ring] 5 times. Tug tail to tighten ring. Finish off leaving a long tail for sewing.

Making the Flower

Leaf (Make 9 – 4 or 5 in each Leaf Color)

ROUND 1 (Right Side) Make a Magic Ring; ch 1, (sc, hdc, dc, picot (*see Special Stitches*) dc, hdc, sc) in ring; DO NOT JOIN. Tug tail to tighten ring. Finish off leaving a long tail for sewing.

Making the Leaf

1. Sew a Leaf to each Flower.

Attaching Leaf to Flower.

2. Position the Flowers and Leaves on the Head Band and sew in place.

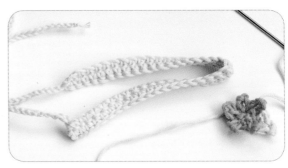

Sewing the Leaves and Flowers to Headband.

Cynthia Doll

CYNTHIA DREAMS OF ONE DAY BEING A PRIMA DONNA
BALLERINA AND PERFORMING ON THE WORLD'S BIGGEST
STAGES. YOU CAN FIND HER MOST DAYS PRACTISING
BALLET IN THE DANCE STUDIO

finished size

About 11¾" (30 cm) tall.

materials

» **DMC Natura Just Cotton**
  » **Main Color (MC)** Ivory (#02) – ¾ oz (25 g); 85 yd (77.5)
  » **Color A** Rose Layette (#06) – ¾ oz (25 g); 85 yd (77.5) for Dress
  » **Color B** Salome (#80) – ¾ oz (25 g); 85 yd (77.5) for Hair

» Size C-2 (2.75 mm) Crochet Hook - or size suitable for yarn used. (Main Hook)
» Size D-3 (3.25 mm) Crochet Hook - for Hair & Skirt

» Black or Dark Grey Embroidery Floss (or Yarn) – for Eyes
» Dark Pink Embroidery Floss (or Yarn) – for Mouth
» Toy Stuffing

» **Note** Use Main Hook throughout, unless otherwise stated.

HEAD

ROUND 1 (Right Side) Starting at the top of the Head, using MC, make a Magic Ring *(see Techniques)*; ch 1, 6 sc in ring; DO NOT JOIN. (6 sc) Tug tail to tighten ring. Mark last stitch.

ROUND 2 [2 sc in next st] around. (12 sc) Move marker each round.

ROUND 3 [Sc in next st, inc *(see Special Stitches)* in next st] around. (18 sc)

ROUND 4 [Sc in each of next 2 sts, inc in next st] around. (24 sc)

ROUND 5 [Sc in each of next 3 sts, inc in next st] around. (30 sc)

ROUND 6 [Sc in each of next 4 sts, inc in next st] around. (36 sc)

ROUNDS 7-9 Sc in each st around. (36 sc)

ROUND 10 Sc in each of next 16 sts, [inc in next st] 3 times, sc in each of next 17 sts. (39 sc)

ROUND 11 Sc in each st around. (39 sc)

ROUND 12 Sc in each of next 18 sts, [inc in next st] 3 times, sc in each of next 18 sts. (42 sc)

ROUNDS 13-14 Sc in each st around. (42 sc)

ROUND 15 Sc in each of next 18 sts, [sc-dec *(see Special Stitches)*] 3 times, sc in each of next 18 sts. (39 sc)

ROUND 16 Sc in each st around. (39 sc)

ROUND 17 Sc in each of next 17 sts, [sc-dec] 3 times, sc in each of next 16 sts. (36 sc)

ROUND 18 Sc in each st around. (36 sc)

ROUND 19 [Sc in each of next 4 sts, sc-dec] around. (30 sc)

ROUND 20 [Sc in each of next 3 sts, sc-dec] around. (24 sc)

Stuff the Head firmly. Do not overstuff the shaped nose. Hint Pinch the nose area while stuffing to avoid over-stuffing and to keep the shape.

ROUND 21 [Sc in each of next 2 sts, sc-dec] around. (18 sc)

ROUNDS 22-24 (Neck) Sc in each st around. (18 sc)

At the end of Round 24, DO NOT FINISH OFF.

BODY and DRESS

ROUND 25 [Sc in each of next 2 sts, inc in next st] around. (24 sc)

ROUND 26 [Sc in each of next 3 sts, inc in next st] around, changing to Color A in last st. (30 sc) Finish off MC.

ROUND 27 With Color A, sc in each st around. (30 sc)

ROUND 28 [Sc in each of next 4 sts, inc in next st] around. (36 sc)

ROUND 29 Sc in each st around. (36 sc)

ROUND 30 [Sc in each of next 5 sts, inc in next st] around. (42 sc)

ROUND 31 Sc in each st around. (42 sc)

ROUND 32 [Sc in each of next 6 sts, inc in next st] around. (48 sc)

ROUNDS 33-47 Sc in each st around. (48 sc)

Stuff the Neck firmly. Start stuffing the Body, making sure the last round can flatten to close.

The finished stuffed Head, Neck and Body.

LAST ROW Working through the double thickness of the flattened Body, sc in each st across (to close), stuffing as you go. (24 sc) Finish off and weave in all ends.

Working across the flattened last round.

ROUND 1 Holding the Doll upside down, with the back of Head facing, using MC and larger hook, working in Round 45 of Body (3 rows up from bottom), insert hook around post of first st from edge, yo and pull up a loop (leaving a 4" tail - 1 loop on hook), ch 1, working around the posts of stitches, sc in each of next 46 sts, working in the round below (to end up where you started), sc in each of last 2 sts; join with sl st to first sc. (48 sts)

Showing where to work in the round below.

ROUND 2 Ch 3 (counts as first dc), 2 dc in same st as joining, dc in each of next 22 sts, 3 dc in next st, dc in each of next 24 sts; join with sl st to first dc (3rd ch of beg ch-3). (52 dc)

Starting the first single crochet of Skirt.

Starting the second round.

ROUND 3 Ch 1, 3 sc in same st as joining, [3 sc in next dc] around; join with sl st to first sc. (156 sc) Finish off and weave in all ends.

First single crochet completed.

Single crochet stitches worked in posts of stitches.

Finished Skirt.

ARMS (Make 2)

ROUND 1 (Right Side) Using MC, make a Magic Ring; ch 1, 8 sc in ring; DO NOT JOIN. (8 sc) Tug tail to tighten ring. Mark last stitch.

ROUNDS 2-5 Sc in each st around. (8 sc) Move marker each round.

At the end of Round 5, change to Color A. Finish off MC.

ROUNDS 6-24 Sc in each st around. (8 sc)

At the end of Round 24, flatten the last round and working through both thicknesses, sc in each of next 4 sc. Finish off leaving a long tail for sewing.

LEGS (Make 2)

ROUND 1 (Right Side) Starting with the shoes, using Color A, make a Magic Ring; ch 1, 10 sc in ring; DO NOT JOIN. (10 sc) Tug tail to tighten ring. Mark last stitch.

ROUNDS 2-5 Sc in each st around. (10 sc) Move marker each round.

At the end of Round 5, change to MC. Finish off Color A.

Start stuffing Legs lightly, adding more as you go.

ROUNDS 6-35 Sc in each st around. (10 sc)

At the end of Round 35, flatten the last round and working through both thicknesses, sc in each of next 5 sc. Finish off leaving a long tail for sewing.

HAIR

ROUND 1 (Right Side) Using Color B and larger hook, make a Magic Ring; ch 1, 6 sc in ring; DO NOT JOIN. (6 sc) Tug tail to tighten ring. Mark last stitch.

ROUND 2 [2 sc in next st] around. (12 sc) Move marker each round.

ROUND 3 [Sc in next st, inc in next st] around. (18 sc)

ROUND 4 [Sc in each of next 2 sts, inc in next st] around. (24 sc)

ROUND 5 [Sc in each of next 3 sts, inc in next st] around. (30 sc)

ROUND 6 [Sc in each of next 4 sts, inc in next st] around. (36 sc)

ROUND 7 [Sc in each of next 5 sts, inc in next st] around. (42 sc)

ROUNDS 8-14 Sc in each st around. (42 sc)

At the end of Round 14, sl st in next st to finish off, leaving a long tail for sewing.

BUNS (Make 2)

ROUND 1 (Right Side) Using Color B and larger hook, make a Magic Ring; ch 1, 8 sc in ring; DO NOT JOIN. (8 sc) Tug tail to tighten ring. Mark last stitch.

ROUND 2 [2 sc in next st] around. (16 sc) Move marker each round.

ROUNDS 3-5 Sc in each st around. (16 sc)

At the end of Round 5, sl st in next st to finish off, leaving a long tail.

SHOULDER CAPE

ROW 1 (Right Side) Leaving a long tail (for first Tie), using MC and larger hook, ch 17; dc in 4th ch from hook (skipped ch count as first dc), [dc in next ch] across. (15 dc)

ROW 2 Ch 3, turn, dc in first st, [2 dc in next st] across, changing to Color A in last st. (30 dc) Finish off MC, leaving a long tail (second Tie) for tying Cape.

ROW 3 Ch 1, turn, sc in each dc across. (30 sc) Finish off Color A and weave in ends.

DOLL ASSEMBLY – Use photo as guide

Arms - Making sure Nose faces forwards, position the Arms slightly to the front on either side of the Body at Round 27. Using long tails and yarn needle, sew them in place.

Legs - Position the Legs along the Last Row of the Body – skipping 5 stitches on either side, and with 4 stitches between them. Using long tails and yarn needle, sew them in place.

Attaching the Arms.

Attaching the Legs.

Hair - Starting at the back of the Head, sew the Hair to the Head.

Bangs - Cut a length of Color B and using Straight Stitches *(see Embroidery Stitches)*, embroider a few strands of hair along the hairline.

Attaching the Hair.

Otis the Donkey

. OTIS IS A YOUNG GARDENER, WHO GETS OUT OF BED EARLY IN THE MORNING. IF YOU'RE LOOKING FOR HIM, YOU WILL FIND HIM TENDING TO HIS VEGETABLE PATCH

finished size

About 10" (25.5 cm) tall – including Ears.

materials

» **DMC Woolly**
  » **Main Color (MC)** Light Grey (#121) – 1 oz (28 g); 78 yd (71 m)
  » **Color A** Off-White (#03) – 1 oz (28 g); 78 yd (71 m) for Muzzle
  » **Color B** Lemon Yellow (#93) – 1 oz (28 g); 78 yd (71 m) for Shirt

» **DMC Natura Just Cotton**
  » **Color C** Rose Layette (#06) – for Cheeks (small amount)

» Size D-3 (3.25 mm) Crochet Hook - or size suitable for yarn used.

» Black or Dark Grey Embroidery Floss (or Yarn) – for Eyes
» Toy Stuffing

HEAD

ROUND 1 (Right Side) Starting with the Muzzle, using Color A, ch 12, 2 sc in 2nd ch from hook, sc in each of next 9 ch, 4 sc in last ch; working in unused lps on other side of starting ch, sc in each of next 9 ch, 2 sc in last ch. DO NOT JOIN. (26 sc) Mark last stitch.

ROUND 2 Inc (see Special Stitches) in first st, sc in each of next 11 sts, [inc in next st] twice, sc in each of next 11 sts, inc in last st. (30 sc) Move marker each round.

ROUND 3 Inc in first st, sc in each of next 13 sts, [inc in next st] twice, sc in each of next 13 sts, inc in last st. (34 sc)

ROUND 4 Inc in first st, sc in each of next 16 sts, inc in next st, sc in each of next 16 sts. (36 sc)

ROUNDS 5-7 Sc in each st around. (36 sc)

At the end of Round 7, change color to MC in last st. Finish off Color A.

ROUNDS 8-17 Sc in each st around. (36 sc)

ROUND 18 [Sc in each of next 4 sts, sc-dec (see Special Stitches)] around. (30 sc)

Start stuffing Head firmly, adding more as you go.

ROUND 19 [Sc in each of next 3 sts, sc-dec] around. (24 sc)

ROUND 20 [Sc in each of next 2 sts, sc-dec] around. (18 sc)

ROUND 21 [Sc in next st, sc-dec] around. (12 sc)

ROUND 22 [Sc-dec] around. (6 sc) Finish stuffing the Head. Fasten off and close (see Techniques).

EARS (Make 2)

ROUND 1 (Right Side) Using MC, make a Magic Ring (see Techniques); ch 1, 6 sc in ring; DO NOT JOIN. (6 sc) Tug tail to tighten ring. Mark last stitch.

ROUND 2 Sc in each st around. (6 sc) Move marker each round.

ROUND 3 [Sc in next st, inc in next st] around. (9 sc)

ROUND 4 Sc in each st around. (9 sc)

ROUND 5 [Sc in each of next 2 sts, inc in next st] around. (12 sc)

ROUNDS 6-14 Sc in each st around. (12 sc)

ROUND 15 [Sc in each of next 2 sts, sc-dec] around. (9 sc)

ROUND 16 [Sc in next st, sc-dec] around. (6 sc) Sl st in next st to finish off, leaving a long tail for sewing.

HEAD ASSEMBLY – Use photo as guide

Holding Head, with Muzzle horizontal, use Floss to embroider the eyes, using Satin Stitch (see Embroidery Stitches) over Rounds 12 &13, with about 8 stitches between them.

Position the Ears about 5 rounds behind the Eyes (about Round 18). Using the long tails and yarn needle, sew in place.

Embroidering the Eyes.

Position of Ears.

LEGS (Make 2)

ROUND 1 (Right Side) Using MC, make a Magic Ring; ch 1, 6 sc in ring; DO NOT JOIN. (6 sc) Tug tail to tighten ring. Mark last stitch.

ROUND 2 [2 sc in next st] around. (12 sc) Move marker each round.

ROUND 3 [Sc in next st, inc in next st] around. (18 sc)

ROUNDS 4-15 Sc in each st around. (18 sc)

At the end of the Round 15 - for the First Leg, finish off. For the Second Leg, DO NOT FINISH OFF.

ROUND 16 (Joining Legs) Ch 3, working on First Leg, sc in last st made (photo #1), sc in each of next 17 sts; working in ch-sts, sc in each of next 3 ch (photo #2); working on Second Leg, sc in each of next 18 sts, working in unused lps on other side of ch, sc in each of next 3 ch. (42 sc) Move marker to last st made (photo #3).

Photo #3

Photo #1

Photo #2

ROUNDS 17-20 Sc in each st around. (42 sc)

At the end of Round 20, change color to Color B in last st. Finish off MC.

ROUNDS 21-27 Sc in each st around. (42 sc)

ROUND 28 [Sc in each of next 5 sts, sc-dec] around. (36 sc)

ROUNDS 29-30 Sc in each st around. (36 sc)

ROUND 31 [Sc in each of next 4 sts, sc-dec] around. (30 sc)

ROUNDS 32-33 Sc in each st around. (30 sc)

ROUND 34 [Sc in each of next 3 sts, sc-dec] around. (24 sc)

ROUNDS 35-36 Sc in each st around. (24 sc)

Start stuffing Legs and Body firmly, adding more as you go.

ROUND 37 [Sc in each of next 2 sts, sc-dec] around. (18 sc) DO NOT FINISH OFF COLOR B. Remove hook from loop.

ROUND 38 Using MC, working in BLO *(see Techniques)* on Round 37, join with sc *(see Techniques)* to first st, [sc in next st] around. (18 sc)

Note Make sure to work in the back loop of the last stitch where Color B is still attached.

Working the Neck using MC in BLO.

ROUND 39 Working in both loops, sc in each st around. (18 sc)

ROUND 40 [Sc in next st, sc-dec] around. (12 sc)

ROUNDS 41-42 Sc in each st around. (12 sc)

At the end of Round 42, sl st in next st to finish off, leaving a long tail for sewing.

Finished Neck.

COLLAR

ROUND 1 Holding the Donkey upside down, pick up Color B's loop, ch 3 (counts as first dc, now and throughout), working in the opposite direction, in the unused front loops of Round 37, dc in same st as joining, dc in each of next 2 sts, [2 dc in next st, dc in each of next 2 sts] around; join with sl st to first dc (3rd ch of beg ch-3). (24 dc)

With Color B, work Collar in the unused front loops.

ROUND 2 Ch 3, [dc in next st] around; join with sl st to first dc (3rd ch of beg ch-3). (24 dc) Finish off and weave in all ends.

Finished Collar.

ARMS (Make 2)

ROUND 1 (Right Side) Using MC, make a Magic Ring; ch 1, 8 sc in ring; DO NOT JOIN. (8 sc) Tug tail to tighten ring. Mark last stitch.

ROUNDS 2-6 Sc in each st around. (8 sc) Move marker each round.

At the end of Round 6, change to Color B. Finish off MC.

ROUNDS 7-18 Sc in each st around. (8 sc)

LAST ROW Flatten the last round and working through both thicknesses, sc in each of next 4 sc. Finish off leaving a long tail for sewing.

CHEEKS (Make 2)

ROUND 1 (Right Side) Using Color C, make a Magic Ring; ch 1, 6 sc in ring; join with sl st to first sc. Finish off leaving a long tail for sewing.

DONKEY ASSEMBLY – Use photo as guide

Attach Head to Body - Position Neck on Head. Sew in place, stuffing the Neck firmly before finishing off.

Sewing Neck onto Head.

Attach Arms - Lift the collar and sew Arms to either side of the Body at Round 36.

Make Mane – Step 1 Wrap Color A about 15-20 times around fingers. (For a thicker mane, add more wraps.)

Step 1

Step 2 Remove wrapped yarn from fingers and cut along one side to make strands of equal length. Reserve a few strands for Tail.

Step 2

Step 3 Holding 2 strands together, fold in half. Insert hook under stitch on top of Donkey's Head between Ears. Place fold of strands on hook and pull half-way through stitch to form a loop.

Step 3

Step 4 Pull tails of strands through the loop and pull tightly to knot.

Step 4

Step 5 Repeat Steps 3 & 4 to cover top and back of Head.

Step 5

Step 6 Trim to desired length.

Step 6

Make Tail Knot the reserved strands (in the same way as for Mane) at the back of the Donkey on Round 20.

Attach Cheeks Position the Cheeks on either side of the Head, about two rounds below the Eyes. Sew in place.

Nova the Giraffe

NOVA IS SUCH A SWEETIE, SHE LOVES TO EAT CAKE AND
SPEND HER TIME GOSSIPING WITH HER FRIENDS AND
HAVING AFTERNOON TEA IN THE SUN

finished size

About 13" (33 cm) tall – including Horns.

materials

» **DMC Woolly**
  » **For Yellow Giraffe**
    » **Main Color (MC)** Cream (#03) – 3½ oz (100 g); 272 yd (250 m)
    » **Color A** Lemon Yellow (#93) – small amounts for Inner Ears & Spots
  » **For Pink Giraffe**
    » **Main Color (MC)** Medium Pink (#42) – 3½ oz (100 g); 272 yd (250 m)
    » **Color A** Pink (#43) – small amounts for Inner Ears & Spots

» Size D-3 (3.25 mm) Crochet Hook - or size suitable for yarn used. (Main Hook)
» Size B-1 (2.25 mm) Crochet Hook – For Inner Ears

» $^{11}/_{32}$" (9 mm) Safety Eyes – 2
» Black or Dark Grey Embroidery Floss (or Yarn) – for Nose
» Toy Stuffing

» **Note** Use Main Hook throughout, unless otherwise stated.

ROUND 1 (Right Side) Starting at the Nose, using MC, make a Magic Ring *(see Techniques)*; ch 1, 6 sc in ring; DO NOT JOIN. (6 sc) Tug tail to tighten ring. Mark last stitch.

ROUND 2 [2 sc in next st] around. (12 sc) Move marker each round.

ROUND 3 [Sc in next st, inc *(see Special Stitches)* in next st] around. (18 sc)

ROUND 4 [Sc in each of next 2 sts, inc in next st] around. (24 sc)

ROUNDS 5-7 Sc in each st around. (24 sc)

ROUND 8 Sc in each of next 11 sts, [inc in next st] 3 times, sc in each of next 10 sts. (27 sc)

ROUND 9 Sc in each st around. (27 sc)

ROUND 10 Sc in each of next 12 sts, [inc in next st] 3 times, sc in each of next 12 sts. (30 sc)

ROUND 11 Sc in each st around. (30 sc)

ROUND 12 Sc in each of next 14 sts, [inc in next st] 3 times, sc in each of next 13 sts. (33 sc)

ROUND 13 Sc in each st around. (33 sc)

ROUND 14 Sc in each of next 15 sts, [inc in next st] 3 times, sc in each of next 15 sts. (36 sc)

ROUND 15 Sc in each st around. (36 sc)

Head showing nose shaping.

ROUND 16 [Sc in each of next 5 sts, inc in next st] around. (42 sc)

ROUND 17 [Sc in each of next 6 sts, inc in next st] around. (48 sc)

ROUND 18 [Sc in each of next 7 sts, inc in next st] around. (54 sc)

ROUNDS 19-26 Sc in each st around. (54 sc)

ROUND 27 [Sc in each of next 7 sts, sc-dec *(see Special Stitches)*] around. (48 sc)

ROUND 28 [Sc in each of next 6 sts, sc-dec] around. (42 sc)

Insert Safety Eyes on either side of nose shaping, between Rounds 18 & 19, about 17 stitches apart.

Positioning the Eyes

ROUND 29 [Sc in each of next 5 sts, sc-dec] around. (36 sc)

ROUND 30 [Sc in each of next 4 sts, sc-dec] around. (30 sc)

Start stuffing Head firmly, adding more as you go.

ROUND 31 [Sc in each of next 3 sts, sc-dec] around. (24 sc)

ROUND 32 [Sc in each of next 2 sts, sc-dec] around. (18 sc)

ROUND 33 [Sc in next st, sc-dec] around. (12 sc)

ROUND 34 [Sc-dec] around. (6 sc). Finish stuffing Head. Fasten off and close *(see Techniques)* but leave a long tail for sewing Eyelids.

Inner Ear (Make 2)

ROW 1 (Right Side) Using Color A and smaller hook, ch 11, sc in 2nd ch from hook, sc in each of next 2 ch, hdc in each of next 3 ch, dc in each of next 3 ch, (2 dc, tr, 2 dc) in last ch; working in unused lps on other side of starting ch, dc in each of next 3 ch, hdc in each of next 3 ch, sc in each of next 3 ch. (23 sts) Finish off.

Outer Ear (Make 2)

ROW 1 (Wrong Side) Using MC and Main Hook, repeat Row 1 of Inner Ear, but DO NOT FINISH OFF. (23 sts)

Ear Assembly Holding an Inner and Outer Ear with wrong sides together, with Outer Ear facing, ch 1, working through both thicknesses using back loops of Outer Ear and front

loops of Inner Ear, matching stitches and shaping, sc in each st across. (23 sc) Finish off leaving a long tail for sewing.

Repeat for other Ear.

Joining Outer and Inner Ears together

ROUND 1 (Right Side) Using MC, make a Magic Ring; ch 1, 8 sc in ring; DO NOT JOIN. (8 sc) Tug tail to tighten ring. Mark last stitch.

ROUNDS 2-8 Sc in each st around. (8 sc) Move marker each round.

At the end of Round 8, sl st in next st. Finish off leaving a long tail for sewing.

Eyelids - Using yarn needle and tail, insert needle from closure, through Head, bringing it out above one Eye (Photo #1). Embroider a few Straight Stitches *(see Embroidery Stitches)* over the eyeball to create eyelids (Photo #2). Insert needle back through Head and repeat for other Eye. Insert needle through Head and bring out at base (where it will be attached to Body). Secure and finish off.

Photo # 1 Bringing needle out at Eye

Photo # 2 Embroidering Eyelids

Ears - Position finished Ears to top of Head in line with the Eyes (about Round 27), and sew in place.

Position of Ears

Horns- Position Horns between the Ears and sew in place.

Nose - Using the Floss, embroider a simple "V" shape, with the point of the V in the center of Magic Ring. Add a little vertical stitch below the V to complete the Nose.

Starting the Nose

BODY

ROUND 1 (Right Side) Starting at base, using MC, repeat Rounds 1-4 of Head.

At the end of Round 4, there are 24 sc.

ROUND 5 [Sc in each of next 3 sts, inc in next st] around. (30 sc)

ROUND 6 [Sc in each of next 4 sts, inc in next st] around. (36 sc)

ROUND 7 [Sc in each of next 5 sts, inc in next st] around. (42 sc)

ROUND 8 [Sc in each of next 6 sts, inc in next st] around. (48 sc)

ROUND 9 [Sc in each of next 7 sts, inc in next st] around. (54 sc)

ROUNDS 10-27 Sc in each st around. (54 sc)

ROUND 28 Sc in each of next 16 sts, [sc-dec, sc in each of next 2 sts] 6 times, sc in each of next 14 sts. (48 sc)

ROUNDS 29-30 Sc in each st around. (48 sc)

ROUND 31 Sc in each of next 13 sts, [sc-dec. sc in each of next 2 sts] 6 times, sc in each of next 11 sts. (42 sc)

ROUNDS 32-33 Sc in each st around. (42 sc)

ROUND 34 Sc in each of next 10 sts, [sc-dec, sc in each of next 2 sts] 6 times, sc in each of next 8 sts. (36 sc)

ROUND 35 Sc in each st around. (36 sc)

ROUND 36 [Sc in each of next 4 sts, sc-dec] around. (30 sc)

ROUND 37 Sc in each st around. (30 sc)

Start stuffing Body firmly, adding more as you go.

ROUND 38 [Sc in each of next 3 sts, sc-dec] around. (24 sc)

ROUNDS 39-60 Sc in each st around. (24 sc)

At the end of Round 60, sl st in next st. Finish off leaving a long tail for sewing.

ARMS (Make 2)

ROUND 1 (Right Side) Using MC, make a Magic Ring; ch 1, 6 sc in ring; DO NOT JOIN. (6 sc) Tug tail to tighten ring. Mark last stitch.

ROUND 2 [2 sc in next st] around. (12 sc) Move marker each round.

ROUND 3 [Sc in next st, inc in next st] around. (18 sc)

ROUND 4 Working in BLO (see Techniques), sc in each st around. (18 sc)

ROUNDS 5-7 Working in both loops, sc in each st around. (18 sc)

ROUNDS 8-13 Sc-dec, [sc in next st] around.

At the end of Round 13, there are 12 sts.

Stuff the Hand firmly and a little way up the Arm.

LAST ROW Flatten the last round and working through both thicknesses, sc in each of next 6 sc to close. Finish off leaving a long tail for sewing.

LEGS (Make 2)

ROUNDS 1-3 Using MC, repeat Rounds 1 to 3 of Arms.

At the end of Round 3, there are 18 sc.

ROUND 4 [Sc in each of next 2 sts, inc in next st] around. (24 sc)

ROUND 5 Working in BLO (see Techniques), sc in each st around. (24 sc)

ROUNDS 6-9 Working in both loops, sc in each st around. (24 sc)

ROUNDS 10-15 Sc-dec, [sc in next st] around.

At the end of Round 15, there are 18 sts.

Start stuffing the Legs, adding more as you go.

ROUNDS 16-37 Sc in each st around. (18 sc)

ROUND 38 [Sc in next st, sc-dec] around. (12 sc)

ROUND 39 [Sc-dec] around. (6 sc) Finish stuffing the Legs. Fasten off and close, leaving a long tail.

GIRAFFE ASSEMBLY – Use photo as guide

Body – Finish stuffing and sew the Head to Neck making sure the Tummy is in the front.

Arms – Using long tails and yarn needle, position the Arms slightly to the front on either side of the Body at about Round 37, and sew in place.

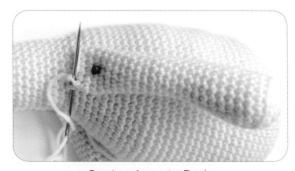

Sewing Arms to Body

Frankie the Bunny

FRANKIE LOVES DRESSING UP IN DIFFERENT COSTUMES.
TODAY HE'S PRETENDING TO BE A NATIVE AMERICAN –
COMPLETE WITH FEATHERS AND WAR PAINT

finished size

About 12″ (30.5 cm) tall – including Ears.

materials

» **DMC Woolly 5**
  » **Main Color (MC)** Natural (#03) – 3½ oz (100 g); 174 yd (160 m)
  » **Color A** Marshmallow (#45) – 1 oz (28 g); 50 yd (45 m) for Inner Ears,
     Paw Pads and Nose

» **DMC Natura Just Cotton**
  » **Color B** Canelle (#37) – small amount for Headband
  » **For Feathers – small amounts of each**
     » **Color C** Ibisa (#01)
     » **Color D** Ble (#83)
     » **Color E** Turquoise (#49)
  » **Face Stripes** Small amounts of Ble (#83), & Turquoise (#49)

» Size E-4 (3.50 mm) Crochet Hook - or size suitable for yarn used. (Main Hook)
» Size G-6 (4.00 mm) Crochet Hook – for Outer Ears
» Size C-2 (2.75 mm) Crochet Hook – for Headband and Feathers

» $^{11}/_{32}$″ (9 mm) Safety Eyes – 2
» Small Pompon maker (optional)
» Toy Stuffing

» **Note** Use Main Hook throughout, unless otherwise stated.

HEAD

ROUND 1 (Right Side) Starting at top of Head, using MC, make a Magic Ring *(see Techniques)*; ch 1, 6 sc in ring; DO NOT JOIN. (6 sc) Tug tail to tighten ring. Mark last stitch.

ROUND 2 [2 sc in next st] around. (12 sc) Move marker each round.

ROUND 3 [Sc in next st, inc *(see Special Stitches)* in next st] around. (18 sc)

ROUND 4 [Sc in each of next 2 sts, inc in next st] around. (24 sc)

ROUND 5 [Sc in each of next 3 sts, inc in next st] around. (30 sc)

ROUND 6 [Sc in each of next 4 sts, inc in next st] around. (36 sc)

ROUND 7 [Sc in each of next 5 sts, inc in next st] around. (42 sc)

ROUND 8 [Sc in each of next 6 sts, inc in next st] around. (48 sc)

ROUND 9 [Sc in each of next 7 sts, inc in next st] around. (54 sc)

ROUNDS 10-24 Sc in each st around. (54 sc)

Insert Safety Eyes between Rounds 16 & 17, about 14 stitches apart.

ROUND 25 [Sc in each of next 7 sts, sc-dec *(see Special Stitches)*] around. (48 sc)

ROUND 26 [Sc in each of next 6 sts, sc-dec] around. (42 sc)

ROUND 27 [Sc in each of next 5 sts, sc-dec] around. (36 sc)

ROUND 28 [Sc in each of next 4 sts, sc-dec] around. (30 sc)

Start stuffing Head firmly, adding more as you go.

ROUND 29 [Sc in each of next 3 sts, sc-dec] around. (24 sc)

ROUND 30 [Sc in each of next 2 sts, sc-dec] around. (18 sc)

ROUND 31 [Sc in next st, sc-dec] around. (12 sc)

ROUND 32 [Sc-dec] around. (6 sc) Finish stuffing Head. Fasten off and close *(see Techniques)* but leave a long tail for sewing Eyelids.

EARS

Inner Ear (Make 2)

ROW 1 (Right Side) Using Color A, ch 17, sc in 2nd ch from hook, sc in each of next 3 ch, hdc in each of next 4 ch, dc in each of next 4 ch, tr in each of next 3 ch, 5 tr in last ch; working in unused lps on other side of starting ch, tr in each of next 3 ch, dc in each of next 4 ch, hdc in each of next 4 ch, sc in each of next 4 ch. (35 sts) Finish off.

Outer Ear (Make 2)

ROUND 1 (Right Side) Using MC and larger hook, repeat Row 1 of Inner Ear, but DO NOT FINISH OFF; join with sl st to first sc (to position yarn for Ear assembly). (35 sts)

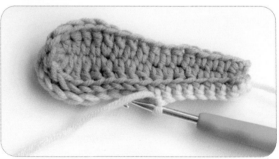

Finishing Outer Ear with slip stitch.

Ear Assembly Holding an Inner and Outer Ear with wrong sides together, with Outer Ear right side facing, ch 1, working through both thicknesses using back loops of Outer Ear and front loops of Inner Ear, matching stitches and shaping, sc in each st across. (35 sc) DO NOT JOIN. Finish off leaving a long tail for sewing.
Repeat for other Ear.

Joining Outer and Inner Ears together

Eyelids – Using yarn needle and tail, insert needle from closure, through Head, bringing it out above one Eye. Embroider two Straight Stitches (see Embroidery Stitches) the length of the eye create an inner eyelid. Insert needle back through Head and repeat for other Eye. Insert needle through Head and bring out at base (where it will be attached to Body). Secure and finish off.

Embroidered Nose.

Embroider inner Eyelids.

Nose – Using Color A and yarn needle, embroider a Nose about 4 rounds below Eyes.

Ears – Position Ears at top of Head about two rounds out from center. Using tails and yarn needle, sew in place.

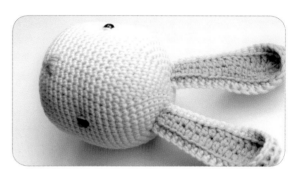

Attached Ears.

BODY

ROUNDS 1-7 Using MC, repeat Rounds 1 to 7 of Head.

At the end of Round 7, there are 42 sc.

ROUNDS 8-15 Sc in each st around. (42 sc)

ROUND 16 [Sc in each of next 5 sts, sc-dec] around. (36 sc)

ROUNDS 17-18 Sc in each st around. (36 sc)

ROUND 19 [Sc in each of next 4 sts, sc-dec] around. (30 sc)

Start stuffing Body firmly, adding more as you go.

ROUNDS 20-21 Sc in each st around. (30 sc)

ROUND 22 [Sc in each of next 3 sts, sc-dec] around. (24 sc)

ROUNDS 23-24 Sc in each st around. (24 sc)

ROUND 25 [Sc in each of next 2 sts, sc-dec] around. (18 sc)

ROUNDS 26-27 Sc in each st around. (18 sc)

At the end of Round 27, sl st in next st. Finish off leaving a long tail for sewing.

FEET (Make 2)

ROUNDS 1-3 Using MC, repeat Rounds 1 to 3 of Head.

At the end of Round 3, there are 18 sc.

ROUNDS 4-11 Sc in each st around. (18 sc)

ROUND 12 [Sc in next st, sc-dec] around. (12 sc)

ROUNDS 13-15 Sc in each st around. (12 sc)

Stuff Feet lightly.

ROUND 16 [Sc-dec] around. (6 sc) Fasten off and close, leaving long tail for sewing.

Paw Pads (Make 2)

ROUNDS 1-2 Using Color A, repeat Rounds 1 to 2 of Head.

At the end of Round 2, sl st in next st to finish off, leaving a long tail for sewing.

ARMS (Make 2)

ROUNDS 1-2 Using MC, repeat Rounds 1 to 2 of Head.

At the end of Round 2, there are 12 sc.

ROUNDS 3-12 Sc in each st around. (12 sc)

ROUND 13 [Sc-dec] around. (6 sc)

Stuff Arm lightly.

LAST ROW Flatten the last round and working through both thicknesses, sc in each of next 3 sc. Finish off leaving a long tail for sewing.

HEADBAND

ROW 1 (Right Side) Using Color B and smaller hook, ch 66, sc in 2nd ch from hook, [sc in next ch] across. (65 sc)

ROWS 2-3 Ch 1, turn, sc in each sc across. (65 sc)

At the end of Row 3, sl st down edge into side of Row 2, ch 40 (First Tie made). Finish off, pulling last st very tight to secure. Weave in ends.

Second Tie
Working on other edge of Headband, join with sl st to side of Row 2, ch 40. Finish off, pulling last st very tight to secure. Weave in all ends.

Feathers (Make 2)

Note When changing colors, carry the unused yarn by working over it.

ROW 1 (Wrong Side) Using Color C and smaller hook, ch 11, sl st in 2nd ch from hook, [sl st in next ch] across. (10 sl sts)

ROW 2 Ch 1, turn, working in BLO, sc in each of next 7 sts, changing to Color D in last st *(see photo #1)*, with Color D, sc in each of next 2 sts, changing to Color E in last st *(see photo #2)*, with Color E, ch 1, 2 dc in last st; working in unused lps on other side of starting ch *(see photo #3)*, 2 dc in first ch, changing to Color D in last st, with Color D, sc in each of next 2 ch, changing to Color C in last st, with Color C, sc in each of next 7 ch, sl st in same ch as last st. Finish off leaving a long tail for sewing.

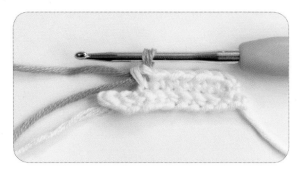

Photo #1 Changing to Color D.

Photo #2 Changing to Color E.

Photo #3 Working in first unused loop of chain.

Finished Feather

Body - Using long tail and yarn needle, sew the Body to the third round of Head, stuffing firmly before closing.

Paw Pads - Using long tail and yarn needle, position Pads on the wider part of the Feet (about Round 4), and sew in place. Embroider 4 toes on each Foot, around top of Pad.

Positioning and sewing Pad Pads to Feet.

Embroidering Toes.

Feet - Using long tail and yarn needle, position Feet to front of Body and sew in place.

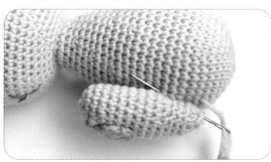

Sewing Feet to Body.

Arms - Position and sew Arms to either side of Body at about Round 27.

Tail - Using Color A, make a pompom and sew to center back of Bunny at about Round 7.

Attaching pompom Tail.

Feathers - Position and sew the Feathers to the inside of the Headband.

Headband - Wrap the Headband around the Head and tie at back of Head.

Face Paint On each cheek, embroider two stripes – one in Color E and one in Color D – for tribal paint marks.

Position of Tribal Stripes.

James the Fox

JAMES IS A DEAR FELLOW AND IS MUCH LOVED BY HIS FRIENDS. HE ALWAYS HAS TIME TO SIT AND LISTEN TO THEM – AND SOMETIMES OFFER HIS ADVICE

finished size

About 14″ (35.5 cm) tall – including Legs and Ears.

materials

» **DMC Woolly 5**
   » **Main Color (MC)** Red (#05) – 1¾ oz (50 g); 87 yd (80 m)
   » **Color A** Natural (#03) – 1 oz (28 g); 50 yd (45 m) for Muzzle
   » **Color B** Black (#02) for Nose – small amount

» Size E-4 (3.50 mm) Crochet Hook - or size suitable for yarn used.

» Small amount black yarn – for Nose
» Black or Dark Grey Embroidery Floss (or Yarn) – for Eyes
» Toy Stuffing

ROUND 1 (Right Side)) Starting at the Muzzle, using Color A, make a Magic Ring *(see Techniques)*; ch 1, 6 sc in ring; DO NOT JOIN. (6 sc) Tug tail to tighten ring. Mark last stitch.

ROUND 2 Sc in each sc around. (6 sc) Move marker each round.

ROUND 3 [2 sc in next st] around. (12 sc)

ROUND 4 Sc in each sc around. (12 sc)

ROUND 5 Sc in each of next 5 sts, [inc *(see Special Stitches)* in next st] 3 times, sc in each of next 4 sts. (15 sc)

ROUND 6 Sc in each sc around. (15 sc)

ROUND 7 Sc in each of next 6 sts, [inc in next st] 3 times, sc in each of next 6 sts. (18 sc)

ROUND 8 Sc in each sc around. (18 sc)

ROUND 9 Sc in each of next 7 sts, [inc in next st] 3 times, sc in each of next 8 sts. (21 sc)

ROUND 10 Sc in each sc around. (21 sc)

ROUND 11 Sc in each of next 9 sts, [inc in next st] 3 times, sc in each of next 9 sts. (24 sc)

ROUND 12 Sc in each sc around. (24 sc)

ROUND 13 Sc in each of next 11 sts, [inc in next st] 3 times, sc in each of next 10 sts. (27 sc)

ROUND 14 Sc in each sc around. (27 sc)

ROUND 15 Sc in each of next 12 sts, [inc in next st] 3 times, sc in each of next 12 sts. (30 sc)

ROUND 16 Sc in each sc around. (30 sc)

ROUND 17 [Sc in each of next 4 sts, inc in next st] around. (36 sc)

ROUND 18 [Sc in each of next 5 sts, inc in next st] around, changing to MC in last st. (42 sc) Finish off Color A.

ROUNDS 19-25 Sc in each sc around. (42 sc)

Hint Mark the 19th st on Round 19, for joining Nose Strip.

ROUND 26 [Sc in each of next 5 sts, sc-dec *(see Special Stitches)*] around. (36 sc)

ROUND 27 [Sc in each of next 4 sts, sc-dec] around. (30 sc) Start stuffing Head firmly, adding more as you go.

ROUND 28 [Sc in each of next 3 sts, sc-dec] around. (24 sc)

ROUND 29 [Sc in each of next 2 sts, sc-dec] around. (18 sc)

ROUND 30 [Sc in next st, sc-dec] around. (12 sc)

ROUND 31 [Sc-dec] around. (6 sc) Finish stuffing the Head. Fasten off and close *(see Techniques)*.

Nose Strip

ROW 1 Holding the Head upside down, using MC, working across center of forehead in Round 19, join with sc *(see Techniques)* around post of marked st, working around posts of sts, sc in each of next 3 sts. (4 sc)

Row 1 of Nose Strip.

ROWS 2-7 Ch 1, turn, sc in each st across. (4 sc)

ROW 8 Ch 1, turn, sc in first st, sc-dec, sc in last st. (3 sc)

ROWS 9-14 Ch 1, turn, sc in each st across. (3 sc)

At the end of Row 19, change to Color B.

ROW 15 With Color B, ch 1, turn, sc in each st across. (3 sc)

Row 15 of Nose Strip.

ROW 16 Ch 1, turn, sc-dec, sc in last st. (2 sc)

ROW 17 Ch 1, turn, sc-dec. (1 sc). Sl st in same last st to finish off, leaving a long tail for sewing.

EARS (Make 2)

ROUND 1 (Right Side) Using MC, make a Magic Ring; ch 1, 6 sc in ring; DO NOT JOIN. (6 sc) Tug tail to tighten ring. Mark last stitch.

ROUND 2 Sc in each st around. (6 sc) Move marker each round.

ROUND 3 [2 sc in next st] around. (12 sc)

ROUND 4 Sc in each st around. (12 sc)

ROUND 5 [Sc in each of next 2 sts, inc in next st] around. (16 sc)

ROUNDS 6-7 Sc in each st around. (16 sc)

LAST ROW Flatten the last round and working through both thicknesses, sc in each of next 8 sc. Finish off leaving a long tail for sewing.

HEAD ASSEMBLY – Use photos as guide

Nose Strip – Using long tail and yarn needle, position Strip down face and sew in place.

Position of Nose Strip on Head.

Ears – Using long tails and yarn needle, position Ears on either side of Nose Strip at Round 27 of Head, and sew in place.

Eyes - Using floss, embroider Sleepy Eyes *(see Embroidery Stitches)* on either side of Nose Strip across Rounds 13 to 15, at a slight angle.

BODY

ROUND 1 (Right Side) Using MC, make a Magic Ring; ch 1, 6 sc in ring; DO NOT JOIN. (6 sc) Tug tail to tighten ring. Mark last stitch.

ROUND 2 [2 sc in next st] around. (12 sc) Move marker each round.

ROUND 3 [Sc in next st, inc in next st] around. (18 sc)

ROUND 4 [Sc in each of next 2 sts, inc in next st] around. (24 sc)

ROUND 5 [Sc in each of next 3 sts, inc in next st] around. (30 sc)

ROUND 6 [Sc in each of next 4 sts, inc in next st] around. (36 sc)

ROUND 7 [Sc in each of next 5 sts, inc in next st] around. (42 sc)

ROUNDS 8-13 Sc in each st around. (42 sc)

ROUND 14 [Sc in each of next 5 sts, sc-dec] around. (36 sc)

ROUNDS 15-16 Sc in each st around. (36 sc)

ROUND 17 [Sc in each of next 4 sts, sc-dec] around. (30 sc)

ROUNDS 18-19 Sc in each st around. (30 sc)

Start stuffing Body firmly, adding more as you go.
ROUND 20 [Sc in each of next 3 sts, sc-dec] around. (24 sc)

ROUNDS 21-27 Sc in each st around. (24 sc)

ROUND 28 [Sc in each of next 2 sts, sc-dec] around. (18 sc)

ROUNDS 29-32 Sc in each st around. (18 sc)

At the end of Round 32, sl st in next st to finish off, leaving a long tail for sewing.

LIMBS (Make 4)

ROUND 1 (Right Side) Using MC, make a Magic Ring; ch 1, 8 sc in ring; DO NOT JOIN. (8 sc) Tug tail to tighten ring. Mark last stitch.

ROUNDS 2-20 Sc in each st around. (8 sc) Move marker each round.

At the end of Round 20, sl st in next st to finish off, leaving a long tail for sewing.

ROUND 1 (Right Side) Using Color A, make a Magic Ring; ch 1, 6 sc in ring; DO NOT JOIN. (6 sc) Tug tail to tighten ring. Mark last stitch.

ROUND 2 Sc in each st around. (6 sc)

ROUND 3 [Sc in next st, inc in next st] around. (9 sc)

ROUND 4 Sc in each st around. (9 sc)

ROUND 5 [Sc in each of next 2 sts, inc in next st] around. (12 sc)

ROUND 6 Sc in each st around. (12 sc)

ROUND 7 [Sc in each of next 3 sts, inc in next st] around. (15 sc)

ROUND 8 Sc in each st around. (15 sc)

ROUND 9 [Sc in each of next 4 sts, inc in next st] around. (18 sc)

ROUND 10 Sc in each st around. (18 sc)

ROUND 11 [Sc in each of next 5 sts, inc in next st] around. (21 sc)

ROUND 12 Sc in each st around. (21 sc)

ROUND 13 [Sc in each of next 6 sts, inc in next st] around. (24 sc)

ROUNDS 14-15 Sc in each st around. (24 sc)

ROUND 16 [Sc in each of next 2 sts, sc-dec] around. (18 sc)

Start stuffing Tail firmly, adding more, only in the Color A part of Tail.

ROUND 17 [Sc in next st, sc-dec] around. (12 sc)

ROUND 18 [Sc in each of next 2 sts, sc-dec] around, changing to MC in last st. (9 sc)

ROUNDS 19-24 With MC, sc in each st around. (9 sc)

At the end of Round 24, sl st in next st to finish off, leaving a long tail for sewing.

FOX ASSEMBLY – Use photo as guide

Attach Body to Head - Position Body to bottom of Head (the front of the neck is on the color change round) and sew in place, stuffing the Neck firmly before finishing off.

Limbs - Position the Arms at either side of the Body at about Round 29 and sew in place. Position Legs to the base of the Body, starting about Round 3, and sew in place.

Tail - Only stuff the tip of Tail (Color A). Flatten the last round and position Tail at back of Body at about Round 7. Using long tail and yarn needle, sew in place. Secure tail by inserting needle through Body, bringing it out about 10 rounds up (photo #1), inserting needle through Tail tip (photo #2), then back into Body and out at base of tail (photo #3). Make a double knot to secure and hide tail inside Body.

Photo #2

Photo #3

Chest Hairs – Using Color A and yarn needle, embroider a few V-stitches to front of Body.

Photo #1

Meadow the Cow

THIS ADORABLE LITTLE COW JUST LOVES HER FOOD, ESPECIALLY THE SWEET STUFF. CANDYFLOSS IS HER FAVE AND SHE LOVES EATING IT FOR BREAKFAST.... SHE MAKES SURE TO BRUSH HER TEETH WELL!

finished size

About 7¾" (20 cm) tall.

materials

» **DMC Natura Just Cotton**
  » **Main Color (MC)** Ivory (#02) – 1½ oz (50 g); 170 yd (155 m)
  » **Color A** Rose Layette (#06) – ¾ oz (25 g); 85 yd (77.5 m) for Muzzle & Hooves
  » **Color B** Bleu Layette (#05) – small amount for Spots and Tail Tie

» Size C-2 (2.75 mm) Crochet Hook - or size suitable for yarn used. (Main Hook)
» Size B-1 (2.25 mm) Crochet Hook – for Inner Ears

» ¹¹/₃₂" (9 mm) Safety Eyes - 2
» ½" (0.25 cm) wide Ribbon - 20" (51 cm) long (to tie around neck)
» Toy Stuffing

Note Use Main Hook throughout, unless otherwise stated.

HEAD

ROUND 1 (Right Side) Starting at Muzzle, using Color A, make a Magic Ring (see Techniques); ch 1, 6 sc in ring; DO NOT JOIN. (6 sc) Tug tail to tighten ring. Mark last stitch.

ROUND 2 [2 sc in next st] around. (12 sc) Move marker each round.

ROUND 3 [Sc in next st, inc (see Special Stitches) in next st] around. (18 sc)

ROUND 4 [Sc in each of next 2 sts, inc in next st] around. (24 sc)

ROUND 5 [Sc in each of next 3 sts, inc in next st] around. (30 sc)

ROUND 6 [Sc in each of next 4 sts, inc in next st] around. (36 sc)

ROUND 7 [Sc in each of next 5 sts, inc in next st] around. (42 sc)

ROUND 8 [Sc in each of next 6 sts, inc in next st] around. (48 sc)

ROUNDS 9-12 Sc in each st around. (48 sc)
At the end of Round 12, change color to MC.

ROUNDS 13-17 With MC, sc in each st around. (48 sc)

ROUND 18 [Sc in each of next 6 sts, sc-dec (see Special Stitches)] around. (42 sc)

ROUNDS 19-20 Sc in each st around. (42 sc)

ROUND 21 [Sc in each of next 5 sts, sc-dec] around. (36 sc)

ROUNDS 22-23 Sc in each st around. (36 sc)

Insert Safety Eyes between Rounds 18 & 19, about 13 stitches apart.

ROUND 24 [Sc in each of next 4 sts, sc-dec] around. (30 sc)

ROUNDS 25-26 Sc in each st around. (30 sc)

Start stuffing Head firmly, adding more as you go.

ROUND 27 [Sc in each of next 3 sts, sc-dec] around. (24 sc)

ROUND 28 [Sc in each of next 2 sts, sc-dec] around. (18 sc)

ROUND 29 [Sc in next st, sc-dec] around. (12 sc)

ROUND 30 [Sc-dec] around. (6 sc) Finish stuffing Head. Fasten off and close (see Techniques).

EARS

Inner Ear (Make 2)

ROUNDS 1-3 (Right Side) Using Color A and smaller hook, repeat Round 1 to 3 of Head. At the end of Round 3, there are 18 sc.

ROUND 4 Sc in next st, inc in next st, [sc in each of next 2 sts, inc in next st] 5 times, sc in last st. (24 sc)

ROUND 5 [Sc in each of next 3 sts, inc in next st] around. (30 sc) Sl st in next st to finish off and weave in ends.

Outer Ear (Make 2)

ROUNDS 1-5 (Right Side) Using MC and Main Hook, repeat Rounds 1 to 5 of Inner Ear, but DO NOT FINISH OFF. (30 sc)

Ear Assembly

Holding an Inner and Outer Ear with wrong sides together,

with Outer Ear facing, working through both thicknesses using back loops of Outer Ear and front loops of Inner Ear, matching stitches, sc in each st around. (30 sc) Sl st in next st to finish off, leaving a long tail for sewing.

Repeat for other Ear.

Joined Inner and Outer Ear

HORNS (Make 2)

ROUND 1 (Right Side) Using MC, make a Magic Ring; ch 1, 8 sc in ring; DO NOT JOIN. (8 sc) Tug tail to tighten ring. Mark last stitch.

ROUNDS 2-5 Sc in each st around. (8 sc) Move marker each round.

At the end of Round 5, sl st in next st to finish off leaving a long tail for sewing.

HEAD ASSEMBLY – Use photos as guide

Ears – Using long tail and yarn needle, fold Ear in half, and sew sides together for about 4 stitches. Repeat on other Ear. Position Ears on either side of Head and sew in place.

Fold Ear and sew together for 4 stitches.

Position Ears and sew in place.

Horns – Position Horns on top of Head between Ears and sew in place.

BODY

ROUNDS 1-8 Using MC, repeat Rounds 1 to 8 of Head.

At the end of Round 8, there are 48 sc.

ROUND 9 [Sc in each of next 7 sts, inc in next st] around. (54 sc)

ROUND 10 [Sc in each of next 8 sts, inc in next st] around. (60 sc)

ROUNDS 11-17 Sc in each st around. (60 sc)

ROUND 18 [Sc in each of next 8 sts, sc-dec] around. (54 sc)

ROUNDS 19-20 Sc in each st around. (54 sc)

ROUND 21 [Sc in each of next 7 sts, sc-dec] around. (48 sc)

ROUNDS 22-23 Sc in each st around. (48 sc)

ROUND 24 [Sc in each of next 6 sts, sc-dec] around. (42 sc)

ROUNDS 25-26 Sc in each st around. (42 sc)

ROUND 27 [Sc in each of next 5 sts, sc-dec] around. (36 sc)

ROUNDS 28-29 Sc in each st around. (36 sc)

ROUND 30 [Sc in each of next 4 sts, sc-dec] around. (30 sc)

ROUNDS 31-32 Sc in each st around. (30 sc)

Start stuffing Body firmly, adding more as you go.

ROUND 33 [Sc in each of next 3 sts, sc-dec] around. (24 sc)

ROUNDS 34-35 Sc in each st around. (24 sc)

ROUND 36 [Sc in each of next 2 sts, sc-dec] around. (18 sc)

ROUNDS 37-40 Sc in each st around. (18 sc) Sl st in next st to finish off, leaving long tail for sewing.

ARMS (Make 2)

ROUNDS 1-2 Using Color A, repeat Rounds 1 to 2 of Head.

At the end of Round 2, there are 12 sc.

ROUND 3 Working in BLO (see Techniques), sc in each st around. (12 sc)

ROUND 4 Working in both loops, sc in each st around, changing to MC in last st. (12 sc)

ROUNDS 5-18 With MC, sc in each st around. (12 sc)

Stuff Arms lightly.

LAST ROW Flatten the last round and working through both thicknesses, sc in each of next 6 sc. Finish off leaving a long tail for sewing.

LEGS (Make 2)

ROUNDS 1-3 Using Color A, repeat Rounds 1 to 3 of Head.

At the end of Round 3, there are 18 sc.

ROUND 4 Working in BLO (see Techniques), sc in each st around. (18 sc)

ROUND 5 Working in both loops, sc in each st around. (18 sc)

ROUND 6 Sc in each st around, changing to MC in last st. (18 sc)

ROUNDS 7-23 With MC, sc in each st around. (12 sc)

Stuff bottom of Legs firmly and top of Legs lightly.

ROUND 24 [Sc in next st, sc-dec] around. (12 sc)

ROUND 25 [Sc-dec] around. (6 sc) Fasten off and close.

Finished stuffed Legs

ROUNDS 1-2 Using Color B, repeat Rounds 1-2 of Head.

At the end of Round 2, there are 12 sc. Sl st in next st to finish off, leaving a long tail.

COW ASSEMBLY – Use photo as guide •••••••••••••••••

Attach Body to Head - Position Body to base of Head and sew in place, stuffing the Neck firmly before finishing off.

Position for sewing on Head.

Arms – Position Arms on either side of the Body, about 10 rounds down from the neck. Using long tails and yarn needle, sew in place.

Legs – Pin Legs in a sitting position on either side at base of Body (at about Round 8). Sew in place, making sure to sew the thighs to the Body to keep the Legs in place.

Pinned Leg position.

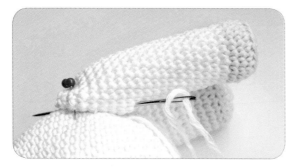

Sewing the thigh to the Body.

Spots – Using long tails and yarn needle, position and sew Spots randomly on the front and back of Body.

Positioning Spots on Body.

Tail – Cut 3 strands of MC, 14" (35.5 cm) long. Fold them in half. Insert hook through stitch at back of Cow (photo #1). Place fold of strands on hook and pull half-way through stitch to form a loop. Pull the tails of strands through the loop and pull tightly to knot (photo # 2). Braid strands together (photo #3) and knot the end securely. Using a strand of Color B, tie a small bow around Tail.

Photo #1

Photo #2

Photo #3

Boris the Bear

BORIS THE BEAR IS A VERY HANDSOME CHAP. HE LIKES
TO LOOK HIS BEST AND KEEPS FIT BY TAKING LONG HIKES
ON A SUNDAY. HE ALWAYS TAKES HIS CAMERA AND HAS
BECOME QUITE THE ACCOMPLISHED PHOTOGRAPHER

finished size

About 8½" (22 cm) tall.

materials

» **DMC Natura Just Cotton**
  » **Main Color** - Ombre (#39) – 1½ oz (50 g); 170 yd (155 m)
  » **Color A** Turquoise (#49) for Sweater - 1½ oz (50 g); 170 yd (155 m)
  » **Color B** Blue Jeans (#26) for stripes – small amount
  » **Color C** Sable (#03) – for Muzzle – small amount

» Size E-4 (3.50 mm) Crochet Hook - or size suitable for yarn used. (Main Hook)
» Size C-2 (2.75 mm) Crochet Hook – for Muzzle

» ¼" (6 mm) Safety Eyes - 2
» Black Embroidery Floss (or Yarn) – for Nose
» Toy Stuffing

Notes

1. Two strands of yarn are held together throughout. Either use two separate balls of same color, or use the center pull and outer pull of same ball.

2. Use Main Hook throughout, unless otherwise stated.

ROUND 1 (Right Side) Starting at top of Head, holding 2 strands of Main Color together, make a Magic Ring *(see Techniques)*; ch 1, 6 sc in ring; DO NOT JOIN. (6 sc) Tug tail to tighten ring. Mark last stitch.

ROUND 2 [2 sc in next st] around. (12 sc) Move marker each round.

ROUND 3 [Sc in next st, inc *(see Special Stitches)* in next st] around. (18 sc)

ROUND 4 [Sc in each of next 2 sts, inc in next st] around. (24 sc)

ROUND 5 [Sc in each of next 3 sts, inc in next st] around. (30 sc)

ROUND 6 [Sc in each of next 4 sts, inc in next st] around. (36 sc)

ROUND 7 [Sc in each of next 5 sts, inc in next st] around. (42 sc)

ROUND 8 [Sc in each of next 6 sts, inc in next st] around. (48 sc)

ROUNDS 9-21 Sc in each st around. (48 sc)

At the end of Round 21, change to Color A.

With marked st on last round as center back, position and insert Safety Eyes on the front, between Rounds 12 & 13, about 11 stitches apart.

ROUNDS 22-36 With Color A, sc in each st around. (48 sc) At the end of Round 36, change to MC.

ROUND 37 With MC, working in BLO *(see Techniques)*, sc in each st around. (48 sc)

ROUNDS 38-40 Sc in each st around. (48 sc) At the end of Round 40, DO NOT FINISH OFF.

LEGS

Flatten the Body. Using stitch markers, mark the 10 stitches at center front and the 10 stitches at center back. The remaining 14 stitches on either side are for the Legs (photo #1). If the yarn is not at the beginning of the first Leg, pull out a few stitches to get there (photo #2). Work around the Leg stitches only (photo #3).

Photo #3

Photo #1

Photo #2

First Leg

ROUND 41 Working around Leg, sc in each of next 14 sts. (14 sc)

ROUNDS 42-46 Sc in each st around. (14 sc)

ROUND 47 [Sc-dec *(see Special Stitches)*] around. (7 sc) Fasten off and close *(see Techniques)*. Stuff first Leg and start stuffing Body firmly.

Second Leg

ROUNDS 41-47 Repeat Rounds 41 to 47 of First Leg. Fasten off and close, leaving a long tail for sewing. Stuff second Leg.

Using long tail and yarn needle, bring the needle up through the Leg to the Body opening. Finish stuffing the Body, and then matching the stitches between the legs, sew the opening closed. Finish off and weave in all ends.

MUZZLE

ROUND 1 (Right Side) Using single strand of Color C and smaller hook, ch 5, 2 sc in 2nd ch from hook, sc in each of next 2 ch, 4 sc in last ch; working in unused lps on other side of starting ch, sc in each of next 2 ch, 2 sc in last ch. DO NOT JOIN. (12 sc) Mark last stitch.

ROUND 2 Inc in first st, sc in each of next 4 sts, [inc in next st] twice, sc in each of next 4 sts, inc in last st. (16 sc)

ROUND 3 Inc in first st, sc in each of next 5 sts, [inc in next st] 4 times, sc in each of next 5 sts, inc in last st. (22 sc) Sl st in next st to finish off, leaving long tail for sewing. Using Floss, embroider a Nose at the wide part of Muzzle *(see photo)*. Position Muzzle between the Eyes about a round below them. Using long end and yarn needle, sew Muzzle in place.

Embroidered Nose and position of Muzzle.

EARS (Make 2)

ROW 1 (Wrong Side) Using MC, make a Magic Ring; ch 1, 6 sc in ring; DO NOT JOIN. (6 sc) Tug tail to tighten ring.

ROW 2 Ch 1, turn, sc in first st, sc in next st, [2 sc in next st] twice, sc in each of next 2 sts. (8 sc) Finish off leaving a long tail for sewing.

Position Ears on either side of Head, about 4 rounds from center. Using long tails and yarn needle, sew in place.

TURTLENECK

ROUND 1 Holding the Bear with the Legs pointing away from you, working in Round 22 (first round of Color A), join with sc *(see Techniques)* to first st, [sc in next st] around. (48 sc)

ROUND 2 Ch 1, dc in each st around; join with sl st to first dc. (48 dc) Finish off and weave in all ends.

Showing where to start Round 1 of Turtleneck.

ARMS (Make 2)

ROUND 1 (Right Side) Using MC, make a Magic Ring; ch 1, 6 sc in ring; DO NOT JOIN. (6 sc) Tug tail to tighten ring. Mark last stitch.

ROUND 2 [2 sc in next st] around. (12 sc) Move marker each round.

ROUNDS 3-5 Sc in each st around. (12 sc)

At the end of Rnd 5, change to Color B.

ROUNDS 6-7 With Color B, sc in each st around. (12 sc)

At the end of Round 7, change to Color A.

ROUNDS 8-9 With Color A, sc in each st around. (12 sc)

ROUNDS 10-13 Rep Rounds 6 to 9 once.

ROUNDS 14-15 Rep Rounds 6 to 7 once more.

Stuff Arms lightly.

LAST ROW Flatten the last round and working through both thicknesses, sc in each of next 6 sc. Finish off leaving a long tail for sewing.

Lift the Turtleneck and position the Arms underneath it, on either side of Body. Using long tails and yarn needle, sew in place.

Working across last row of Arm.

Attaching the finished Arms.

Luka the Lion

LUKA THE LION IS DESTINED TO BE KING OF THE JUNGLE
ONE DAY WHEN HE GROWS UP. HE'S VERY ECOLOGICALLY
AWARE AND LOVES SHOWING HIS FRIENDS HOW TO CARE
FOR POTTED PLANTS

finished size

About 13" (33 cm) tall.

materials

» **DMC Woolly**
  » **Main Color (MC)** Cream (#03) – 3½ oz (100 g); 272 yd (250 m)
  » **Color A** Lemon Yellow (#93) – small amount for Mane
  » **Color B** Pale Yellow (#92) – small amount for Nose Strip

» Size D-3 (3.25 mm) Crochet Hook - or size suitable for yarn used.

» Black Embroidery Floss (or Yarn) – for Eyes & Nose
» Toy Stuffing

PATTERN STITCHES

2 dc Bobble (2dc-bob) Yarn over, insert hook in stitch or space indicated and draw up a loop (3 loops on hook), yarn over, pull through 2 loops on hook (2 loops on remain on hook), yarn over, insert hook in same stitch or space and draw up a loop, yarn over, pull through 2 loops on hook (3 loops remain on hook), yarn over, pull through all 3 loops on hook.

3dc Bobble (3dc-bob): Yarn over, insert hook in stitch or space indicated and draw up a loop (3 loops on hook), yarn over, pull through 2 loops on hook (2 loops on remain on hook), *yarn over, insert hook in same stitch or space and draw up a loop, yarn over, pull through 2 loops on hook; repeat from * once more (4 loops remain on hook), yarn over, pull through all 4 loops on hook.

HEAD

ROUND 1 (Right Side) Starting at top of Head, using MC, make a Magic Ring *(see Techniques)*; ch 1, 6 sc in ring; DO NOT JOIN. (6 sc) Tug tail to tighten ring. Mark last stitch.

ROUND 2 [2 sc in next st] around. (12 sc) Move marker each round.

ROUND 3 [Sc in next st, inc *(see Special Stitches)* in next st] around. (18 sc)

ROUND 4 [Sc in each of next 2 sts, inc in next st] around. (24 sc)

ROUND 5 [Sc in each of next 3 sts, inc in next st] around. (30 sc)

ROUND 6 [Sc in each of next 4 sts, inc in next st] around. (36 sc)

ROUND 7 [Sc in each of next 5 sts, inc in next st] around. (42 sc)

ROUND 8 [Sc in each of next 6 sts, inc in next st] around. (48 sc)

ROUND 9 [Sc in each of next 7 sts, inc in next st] around. (54 sc)

ROUNDS 10-22 Sc in each st around. (54 sc)

ROUND 23 [Sc in each of next 7 sts, sc-dec *(see Special Stitches)*] around. (48 sc)

ROUND 24 [Sc in each of next 6 sts, sc-dec] around. (42 sc)

ROUND 25 [Sc in each of next 5 sts, sc-dec] around. (36 sc)

ROUND 26 [Sc in each of next 4 sts, sc-dec] around. (30 sc)

Start stuffing Head firmly, adding more as you go.

ROUND 27 [Sc in each of next 3 sts, sc-dec] around. (24 sc)

ROUND 28 [Sc in each of next 2 sts, sc-dec] around. (18 sc)

ROUND 29 [Sc in next st, sc-dec] around. (12 sc)

ROUND 30 [Sc-dec] around. (6 sc) Finish stuffing the Head. Fasten off and close *(see Techniques)*.

NOSE STRIP

ROW 1 (Right Side) Using Color B, ch 19, sc in 2nd ch from hook, [sc in next ch] across. (18 sc)

ROWS 2-3 Ch 1, turn, sc in each st across. (18 sc)

At the end of Row 3, finish off leaving a long tail for sewing.

MANE

ROW 1 (Right Side) Starting with a long tail (for sewing sides together), using Color A, ch 56, 2dc-bob *(see Pattern Stitches)* in 4th ch from hook (skipped ch count as first dc), ch 1, skip next ch, 3dc-bob *(see Pattern Stitches)* in next ch, [ch 1, skip next ch, 3dc-bob in next ch] across. (27 bobbles)

Row 1 – First bobble made.

After finishing Row 1.

ROW 2 Ch 1, turn, sc in first st, [sc in next ch-1 sp, sc in next st] across, ending with sc in last dc (3rd ch of skipped ch-3). (54 sc)

ROW 3 Ch 3, turn, skip first st, [2dc-bob in next st, ch 1, skip next st] across, ending with 3dc-bob in last st. (27 bobbles)

Row 3 – Working first bobble in second stitch.

ROW 4 Ch 1, turn, fold the first row up in front of the 3rd row, working through the unused loops of starting ch together with stitches from Row 3, matching sts, sc in each st and ch across. (54 sc) Finish off leaving a long tail for sewing Mane to Head.

Working through both starting chain and stitches from Row 3.

Row 4 - Half-way through Row 4.

Using starting tail and yarn needle, sew sides together to form a ring.

Sides sewn together to form a ring.

EARS (Make 2)

ROUND 1 (Right Side) Using MC, make a Magic Ring; ch 1, 6 sc in ring; DO NOT JOIN. (6 sc) Tug tail to tighten ring. Mark last stitch.

ROUND 2 [Sc in next st, inc in next st] around. (9 sc) Move marker each round.

ROUND 3 Sc in each st around. (9 sc)

ROUND 4 [Sc in each of next 2 sts, inc in next st] around. (12 sc)

ROUNDS 5-6 Sc in each st around. (12 sc)

LAST ROW Flatten the last round and working through both thicknesses, sc in each of next 6 sc. Finish off leaving a long tail for sewing.

HEAD ASSEMBLY – Use photos as guide

Nose Strip – Pin Nose Strip down, starting from center at top of Head (photo #1) and sew in place (photo #2).

Photo #1

Photo #2

Mane - Position the Mane around the Head and pin in place. The Mane goes over the center top (by the Nose Strip) and then under the "chin" – not at center base – at about round 5. Sew the Mane around the Head.

Side view of Mane Placement.

Mane pinned in place.

Sewing Mane around Head.

LIMBS (Make 4)

ROUND 1 (Right Side) Using MC, make a Magic Ring; ch 1, 6 sc in ring; DO NOT JOIN. (6 sc) Tug tail to tighten ring. Mark last stitch.

ROUND 2 [2 sc in next st] around. (12 sc) Move marker each round.

ROUNDS 3-7 Sc in each st around. (12 sc)

ROUND 8 [Sc in each of next 2 sts, sc-dec] around. (9 sc)

Stuff the Hands & Feet lightly.

ROUNDS 9-26 Sc in each st around. (9 sc)

At the end of Round 26, sl st in next st to finish off, leaving a long tail for sewing.

Ears – Pin Ears in front of Mane on either side of Nose Strip and sew in place.

Position of Ears.

Face – Using Floss, embroider the Eyes on either side, in line with the bottom of the Nose Strip. For the Nose, embroider a few stitches over the end of the Nose Strip.

Embroidering Eyes and Nose.

BODY

ROUNDS 1-9 Using MC, repeat Rounds 1 to 9 of Head.

At the end of Round 9, there are 54 sc.

ROUNDS 10-17 Sc in each st around. (54 sc)

ROUND 18 [Sc in each of next 7 sts, sc-dec] around. (48 sc)

ROUNDS 19-20 Sc in each st around. (48 sc)

ROUND 21 [Sc in each of next 6 sts, sc-dec] around. (42 sc)

ROUNDS 22-23 Sc in each st around. (42 sc)

ROUND 24 [Sc in each of next 5 sts, sc-dec] around. (36 sc)

ROUNDS 25-26 Sc in each st around. (36 sc)

ROUND 27 [Sc in each of next 4 sts, sc-dec] around. (30 sc)

ROUNDS 28-29 Sc in each st around. (30 sc)

Start stuffing Body firmly, adding more as you go.

ROUND 30 [Sc in each of next 3 sts, sc-dec] around. (24 sc)

ROUNDS 31-32 Sc in each st around. (24 sc)

ROUND 33 [Sc in each of next 2 sts, sc-dec] around. (18 sc)

ROUNDS 34-35 Sc in each st around. (18 sc)

At the end of Round 35, sl st in next st to finish off, leaving a long tail for sewing.

TAIL

ROUND 1 (Right Side) Using Color A, make a Magic Ring; ch 1, 6 sc in ring; DO NOT JOIN. (6 sc) Tug tail to tighten ring. Mark last stitch.

ROUND 2 Sc in each st around. (6 sc)

ROUND 3 [Sc in next st, inc in next st] around. (9 sc)

ROUND 4 Sc in each st around. (9 sc)

ROUND 5 [Sc in each of next 2 sts, inc in next st] around. (12 sc)

ROUND 6 Sc in each st around. (12 sc)

ROUND 7 [Sc in each of next 2 sts, sc-dec] around. (9 sc)

ROUND 8 [Sc in next st, sc-dec] around, changing to MC in last st. (6 sc)

Stuff Tail tip firmly (only the Color A part of Tail).

Hint For the remaining rounds, it might be easier to remove the marker and just count the rounds on the Tail.

ROUNDS 9-22 With MC, sc in each st around. (6 sc)

At the end of Round 22, sl st in next st to finish off, leaving a long tail for sewing.

LION ASSEMBLY – Use photo as guide

Attach Body to Head - Position Body to bottom of Head at Round 3. Using long tail and yarn needle, sew in place, stuffing the Neck firmly before finishing off.

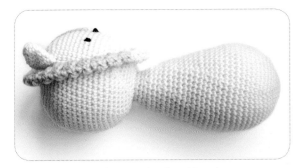

Body attached to Head.

Limbs – Position the Arms at either side of the Body at about Round 33. Using long tails and yarn needle, sew in place.

Position the Legs toward front of Body at Round 6, with about 5 stitches between them. Using long tails and yarn needle, sew in place.

Tail – Position the Tail at back of Body at about Round 9. Using long tail and yarn needle, sew in place.

Position of Tail.

Scarlett

SCARLETT IS A CHATTERBOX. SHE LOVES NOTHING MORE
THAN TALKING FOR HOURS WITH HER FRIENDS AND SHE
RUNS UP QUITE THE PHONE BILL. A VERY SOCIAL GIRL
WHO IS LOVING, KIND AND ALWAYS THERE WHEN NEEDED

finished size

About 10″ (25.5 cm) tall.

materials

» **DMC Natura Just Cotton**
  » **Main Color (MC)** Ivory (#02) – 1½ oz (50 g); 170 yd (155 m)
  » **Color A** Gris Argent (#09) – small amount for Boots
  » **Color B** Rose Layette (#06) – small amount for Cheeks

» **DMC Woolly**
  » **Color C** Medium Pink (#042) – 1 oz (28 g); 78 yd (71 m) for Dress
  » **Color D** Off-White (#01) – 1small amount for Dress (optional).
  » **Color E** Pale Yellow (#092) – small amount for Hair

» Size C-2 (2.75 mm) Crochet Hook - or size suitable for yarn used. (Main Hook)
» Size E-4 (3.50 mm) Crochet Hook - for Hair & Dress

» Black or Dark Grey Embroidery Floss (or Yarn) - for Eyebrows
» ¼″ (6 mm) Safety Eyes - 2
» Toy Stuffing

» **Note** Use Main Hook throughout, unless otherwise stated.

Center Single Crochet (or Waistcoat Stitch) (c-sc)
(See Diagram) This is a variation of the single crochet stitch and looks similar to the knitted stockinette stitch. Instead of inserting the hook under the front and back loops of the stitches on the previous row – as for a normal single crochet – insert the hook between the "legs" or "upside-down V" of the stitch on the previous row. The stitch is completed as usual – draw up a loop, yarn over and pull through both loops on hook.

Hint This stitch is easier to do when worked loosely.

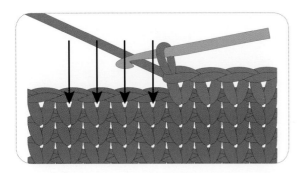

Diagram showing where to insert hook for Center Single Crochet.

Creating Color D "V"s (v-sc) Working in Center Single Crochet stitch, insert hook in indicated stitch, draw up a loop in Color D (photo #1), but finish the stitch in Color C – yarn over, draw through both loops on hook (photo #2).

Photo #1

Photo #2

ROUND 1 (Right Side) Starting at the top of the Head, using MC, make a Magic Ring *(see Techniques)*; ch 1, 6 sc in ring; DO NOT JOIN. (6 sc) Tug tail to tighten ring. Mark last stitch.

ROUND 2 [2 sc in next st] around. (12 sc) Move marker each round.

ROUND 3 [Sc in next st, inc *(see Special Stitches)* in next st] around. (18 sc)

ROUND 4 [Sc in each of next 2 sts, inc in next st] around. (24 sc)

ROUND 5 [Sc in each of next 3 sts, inc in next st] around. (30 sc)

ROUND 6 [Sc in each of next 4 sts, inc in next st] around. (36 sc)

ROUND 7 [Sc in each of next 5 sts, inc in next st] around. (42 sc)

ROUND 8 [Sc in each of next 6 sts, inc in next st] around. (48 sc)

ROUNDS 9-20 Sc in each st around. (48 sc)

ROUND 21 [Sc in each of next 6 sts, sc-dec *(see Special Stitches)*] around. (42 sc)

ROUND 22 [Sc in each of next 5 sts, sc-dec] around. (36 sc)

Insert Safety Eyes between Rounds 15 & 16, about 14 stitches apart.

ROUND 23 [Sc in each of next 4 sts, sc-dec] around. (30 sc)

Start stuffing Head firmly, adding more as you go.

ROUND 24 [Sc in each of next 3 sts, sc-dec] around. (24 sc)

ROUND 25 [Sc in each of next 2 sts, sc-dec] around. (18 sc)

ROUND 26 [Sc in next st, sc-dec] around. (12 sc)

ROUND 27 [Sc-dec] around. (6 sc) Finish stuffing the Head. Fasten off and close *(see Techniques)*.

Finished Head.

LEGS (Make 2)

ROUND 1 (Right Side) Using MC, make a Magic Ring; ch 1, 6 sc in ring; DO NOT JOIN. (6 sc) Tug tail to tighten ring. Mark last stitch.

ROUND 2 [2 sc in next st] around. (12 sc) Move marker each round.

ROUND 3 [Sc in next st, inc in next st] around. (18 sc)

ROUNDS 4-30 Sc in each st around. (18 sc)

At the end of the Round 30 - for the First Leg, finish off. For the Second Leg, DO NOT FINISH OFF.

BODY

ROUND 31 (Joining Legs) Ch 3, working on First Leg, sc in last st made, sc in each of next 17 sts; working in ch-sts, sc in each of next 3 ch; working on Second Leg, sc in each of next 18 sts, working in unused lps on other side of ch-3, sc in each of next 3 ch. (42 sc) Move marker to last st made.

ROUNDS 32-40 Sc in each st around. (42 sc)

ROUND 41 [Sc in each of next 5 sts, sc-dec] around. (36 sc)

ROUNDS 42-43 Sc in each st around. (36 sc)

ROUND 44 [Sc in each of next 4 sts, sc-dec] around. (30 sc)

ROUNDS 45-46 Sc in each st around. (30 sc)

Start stuffing Legs and Body firmly, adding more as you go.

ROUND 47 [Sc in each of next 3 sts, sc-dec] around. (24 sc)

ROUNDS 48-49 Sc in each st around. (24 sc)

ROUND 50 [Sc in each of next 2 sts, sc-dec] around. (18 sc)

ROUNDS 51-52 Sc in each st around. (18 sc)

ROUND 53 [Sc in next st, sc-dec] around. (12 sc)

ROUNDS 54-55 Sc in each st around. (12 sc)

At the end of Round 55, slip stitch in next st to finish off, leaving a long tail for sewing.

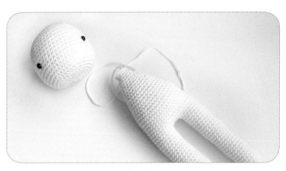

Finished Body.

ARMS (Make 2)

ROUND 1 (Right Side) Using MC, make a Magic Ring; ch 1, 8 sc in ring; DO NOT JOIN. (8 sc) Tug tail to tighten ring. Mark last stitch.

ROUNDS 2-22 Sc in each st around. (8 sc) Move marker each round.

LAST ROW Flatten the last round and working through both thicknesses, sc in each of next 4 sc. Finish off leaving a long tail for sewing.

BODY ASSEMBLY – Use photo as guide

Body - Using long tail and yarn needle, sew the Body to the second round of Head, stuffing firmly before closing.

Arms – Position Arms on either side of Body at Round 53 and sew in place.

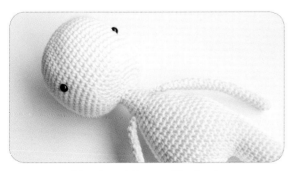

Head and Arms attached.

HAIR

ROUNDS 1-7 Using Color E and larger hook, repeat Rounds 1 to 7 of Head. At the end of Round 7, there are 42 sc.

ROUNDS 8-13 Sc in next st around. (42 sc)

ROUND 14 Hdc in each of next 3 sts, dc in each of next 5 sts, hdc in each of next 3 sts, sc in each of next 21 sts, hdc in each of next 4 sts, dc in each of next 3 sts, skip next st, sl st in each of next 2 sts. Finish off leaving a long tail for sewing.

Finished Hair

HAIR ASSEMBLY – Use photo as guide

Place the Hair on Head, with the sc-sts at the back of Head and the hdc- and dc-sts to the front, with the small parting in the bangs slightly to the left hand side. Using long end and yarn needle, sew in place.

Sewing Hair to Head.

Braids – Cut 12 lengths of Color E – each 12″ long, giving you six pairs of 2 strands each (photo #1). Using one pair at a time, fold strands in half. Insert hook through a stitch at side of Head (photo #2). Place fold of strands on hook and pull half-way through stitch to form a loop. Pull the tails of strands through the loop and pull tightly to knot (photo # 3). Repeat using 3 pairs of strands on either side of Head (photo #4). Braid the strands together and knot the ends securely. Using a strand of MC, tie a small bow around braids (photo #5). Trim the ends.

Photo #1

Photo #2

CHEEKS (Make 2)

ROUND 1 (Right Side) Using Color B, make a Magic Ring; ch 1, 8 sc in ring; join with sl st to first sc.

Finish off leaving a long tail for sewing.

Photo #3

Photo #4

Photo #5

FACE ASSEMBLY – Use photo as guide

Cheeks – Using long tails and yarn needle, position the Cheeks under the Eyes towards the hairline, and sew in place.

Eyebrows – Using Floss, embroider a straight stitch above each Eye.

Nose – Using MC, embroider 2 small stitches in the center of face, on the round below the Eyes.

Finished Face.

Bottom Ribbing

ROW 1 Using Color C and larger hook, ch 5, sc in 2nd ch from hook, [sc in next ch] across. (4 sc)

ROWS 2-35 Ch 1, turn, working in BLO (see Techniques), sc in each st across. (4 sc)

ROW 36 (Joining Row) Ch 1, turn, holding the unused loops of starting ch behind last row, working through both thicknesses (BLO of Row 35), sc in each st across. (4 sc) DO NOT FINISH OFF.

Joining Row - to form a ring.

Dress

ROUND 1 (Right Side) Ch 1, working in sides of ribbing rows (photo #1), sc in each row around (photo #2). DO NOT JOIN. (36 sc) Mark last stitch.

Photo #1

Photo #2

ROUND 2 C-sc (see Pattern Stitches) in each st around. (36 sc) Move marker each round.

After Round 2 - showing the "stockinette" look.

Notes

1. For Rounds 3-19, if using both colors, crochet over or "carry" Color D when not being used.

2. From Round 4 to Round 19, position and make the "V"s between the "V"s on the previous round. If needed, adjust the stitches.

ROUND 3 [C-sc in each of next 5 sts, v-sc (see Pattern Stitches) in next st] around. (36 sc)

ROUND 4 (see Note 2) C-sc in each of next 2 sts, [v-sc in next st, c-sc in each of next 5 sts] around, ending with v-sc in next st, c-sc in each of next 3 sts. (36 sc)

ROUNDS 5-16 Repeat Rounds 3 to 4 six times.

ROUND 17 Sc-dec, c-sc in each of next 32 sts, sc-dec. (34 sc)

ROUND 18 Sc-dec, c-sc in each of next 30 sts, sc-dec. (32 sc)

ROUND 19 Sc-dec, c-sc in each of next 30 sts, sc-dec. (30 sc) Finish off Color D (work over it for a few stitches to secure it).

ROUND 20 With Color C, c-sc in each st around. (30 sc)

ROUND 21 (Armholes) C-sc in each of next 6 sts, ch 5, skip next 5 sts, c-sc in each of next 8 sts, ch 5, skip next 5 sts, c-sc in each of next 6 sts. (20 sc & 2 ch-5 loops)

End of Round 21 – Armholes made.

ROUND 22 Working in regular sc-stitch, sc in each of next 6 sts, 6 sc in next ch-5 lp, sc in each of next 8 sc, 6 sc in each of next ch-5 lp, sc in each of next 6 sts. (32 sc)

ROUND 23 (Cowl Neck) Turn the Dress upside down, to work in opposite direction (photo #1), ch 3, [dc in next st] around; join with sl st to first dc (3rd ch of beg ch-3). (32 dc) Finish off and weave in all ends.

Working the Cowl Neck.

Finished Cowl Neck.

BOOTS (Make 2)

ROUNDS 1-3 Using Color A, repeat Rounds 1 to 3 of Legs.

At the end of Round 3, there are 18 sc.

ROUND 4 [2 dc in next st] 3 times, sc in each of next 15 sts. (6 dc & 15 sc)

ROUNDS 5-7 Sc in each st around. (21 sc)

ROUND 8 Sc in each of next 2 sts, [sc-dec] twice, sc in each of next 15 sts. (19 sc)

ROUNDS 9-13 Sc in each st around. (19 sc)

At the end of Round 13, sl st in next 2 sts to finish off. Weave in all ends.

DOLL ASSEMBLY – use photo as guide

Pull the Dress up over the Legs onto the Body and slip the Arms into the armholes.

Place the Boots on the Feet.

Kobi the Crocodile

AS WITH MOST CROCODILES, KOBI LOVES THE WATER.
HE SPENDS HIS SPARE TIME ENJOYING LOTS OF WATER
SPORTS ESPECIALLY SURFING AND IS CURRENTLY SAVING
UP FOR HIS VERY OWN JET SKI

finished size

About 8″ (20.5 cm) tall.

Materials

» **DMC Natura Just Cotton**
  » **Main Color (MC)** Light Green (#12) – 1½ oz (50 g); 170 yd (155 m)
  » **Color A** Bleu Layette (#05) – ¾ oz (25 g); 85 yd (77.5 m) for Sweater
  » **Color B** Rose Layette (#06) – for Cheeks (small amount)

» Size C-2 (2.75 mm) Crochet Hook - or size suitable for yarn used. (Main Hook)

» $^{11}/_{32}$″ (9 mm) Safety Eyes – 2
» Small buttons for Sweater - 2
» Toy Stuffing

HEAD

ROUND 1 (Right Side) Starting at tip of jaw, using MC, ch 7, 2 sc in 2nd ch from hook, sc in each of next 4 ch, 4 sc in last ch; working in unused lps on other side of starting ch, sc in each of next 4 ch, 2 sc in last ch. DO NOT JOIN. (16 sc) Mark last stitch.

ROUND 2 Sc in each st around. (16 sc)

ROUND 3 Inc *(see Special Stitches)* in first st, sc in each of next 6 sts, [inc in next st] twice, sc in each of next 6 sts, inc in last st. (20 sc) Move marker each round.

ROUNDS 4-5 Sc in each st around. (20 sc)

ROUND 6 Inc in first st, sc in each of next 8 sts, [inc in next st] twice, sc in each of next 8 sts, inc in last st. (24 sc)

ROUNDS 7-10 Sc in each st around. (24 sc)

ROUND 11 [Sc in each of next 3 sts, inc in next st] around. (30 sc)

ROUND 12 Sc in each st around. (30 sc)

ROUND 13 [Sc in each of next 4 sts, inc in next st] around. (36 sc)

ROUND 14 Sc in each st around. (36 sc)

ROUND 15 [Sc in each of next 5 sts, inc in next st] around. (42 sc)

ROUNDS 16-21 Sc in each st around. (42 sc)

ROUND 22 [Sc in each of next 5 sts, sc-dec *(see Special Stitches)*] around. (36 sc)

ROUND 23 [Sc in each of next 4 sts, sc-dec] around. (30 sc)

ROUND 24 [Sc in each of next 3 sts, sc-dec] around. (24 sc)

Start stuffing Head firmly, adding more as you go.

ROUND 25 [Sc in each of next 2 sts, sc-dec] around. (18 sc)

ROUND 26 [Sc in next st, sc-dec] around. (12 sc)

ROUND 27 [Sc-dec] around. (6 sc) Finish stuffing the Head. Fasten off and close *(see Techniques)*.

EYE SOCKETS (Make 2)

ROUND 1 (Right Side) Using MC, make a Magic Ring *(see Techniques)*; ch 1, 6 sc in ring; DO NOT JOIN. (6 sc) Tug tail to tighten ring. Mark last stitch.

ROUND 2 [2 sc in next st] around. (12 sc) Move marker each round.

ROUNDS 3-5 Sc in each st around. (12 sc)

At the end of Round 5, sl st in next st to finish off, leaving a long end for sewing.

CHEEKS (Make 2)

ROUND 1 (Right Side) Using Color B, make a Magic Ring; ch 1, 6 sc in ring; join with sl st to first sc. Finish off leaving a long tail for sewing.

HEAD ASSEMBLY – Use photo as guide

Eyes – Insert the safety eyes between Rounds 3 and 4 of the Eye Socket, securing them of the inside. Position Eye Sockets on top of Head about Round 18, with 6 stitches between them. Using long tails and yarn needle, sew in place.

Eye Sockets pinned in place.

Cheeks – Position Cheeks on either side of Head, about 2 stitches below the Eye Sockets. Using long tails and yarn needle, sew in place.

LEGS (Make 2)

ROUND 1 (Right Side) Using MC, make a Magic Ring; ch 1, 6 sc in ring; DO NOT JOIN. (6 sc) Tug tail to tighten ring. Mark last stitch.

ROUND 2 [2 sc in next st] around. (12 sc) Move marker each round.

ROUND 3 [Sc in next st, inc in next st] around. (18 sc)

ROUNDS 4-15 Sc in each st around. (18 sc)

At the end of the Round 15 - for the First Leg, finish off. For the Second Leg, DO NOT FINISH OFF.

BODY

ROUND 16 (Joining Legs) Ch 3, working on First Leg, sc in last st made, sc in each of next 17 sts; working in ch-sts, sc in each of next 3 ch; working on Second Leg, sc in each of next 18 sts, working in unused lps on other side of ch, sc in each of next 3 ch. (42 sc) Move marker to last st made.

ROUNDS 17-20 Sc in each st around. (42 sc)

At the end of Round 20, change color to Color A in last st. Finish off MC.

ROUNDS 21-27 Sc in each st around. (42 sc)

ROUND 28 [Sc in each of next 5 sts, sc-dec] around. (36 sc)

ROUNDS 29-30 Sc in each st around. (36 sc)

ROUND 31 [Sc in each of next 4 sts, sc-dec] around. (30 sc)

ROUNDS 32-33 Sc in each st around. (30 sc)

ROUND 34 [Sc in each of next 3 sts, sc-dec] around. (24 sc)

ROUNDS 35-36 Sc in each st around. (24 sc)

Start stuffing Legs and Body firmly, adding more as you go.

ROUND 37 [Sc in each of next 2 sts, sc-dec] around. (18 sc) DO NOT FINISH OFF COLOR B. Remove hook from loop.

NECK

ROUND 38 Using MC, working in BLO (*see Techniques*) on Round 37, join with sc (*see Techniques*) to first st, [sc in next st] around. (18 sc)

Working the Neck using MC in BLO.

Note Make sure to work in the back loop of the last stitch where Color B is still attached.

ROUND 39 Working in both loops, sc in each st around. (18 sc)

ROUND 40 [Sc in next st, sc-dec] around. (12 sc)

ROUNDS 41-42 Sc in each st around. (12 sc)

At the end of Round 42, sl st in next st to finish off, leaving a long tail for sewing.

COLLAR

ROUND 1 Holding the Body upside down, pick up Color B's loop, ch 3 (counts as first dc, now and throughout), working in the opposite direction, in the unused front loops of Round 37, dc in same st as joining, dc in each of next 2 sts, [2 dc in next st, dc in each of next 2 sts] around; join with sl st to first dc (3rd ch of beg ch-3). (24 dc)

ROUND 2 Ch 3, [dc in next st] around; join with sl st to first dc (3rd ch of beg ch-3). (24 dc) Finish off and weave in all ends.

Working Collar in the unused front loops.

ARMS (Make 2)

ROUND 1 (Right Side) Using MC, make a Magic Ring; ch 1, 8 sc in ring; DO NOT JOIN. (8 sc) Tug tail to tighten ring. Mark last stitch.

ROUNDS 2-6 Sc in each st around. (8 sc) Move marker each round.

At the end of Round 6, change to Color A. Finish off MC.

ROUNDS 7-19 Sc in each st around. (8 sc)

LAST ROW Flatten the last round and working through both thicknesses, sc in each of next 4 sc. Finish off leaving a long tail for sewing.

ROUND 1 (Right Side) Using MC, make a Magic Ring; ch 1, 6 sc in ring; DO NOT JOIN. (6 sc) Tug tail to tighten ring. Mark last stitch.

ROUND 2 Sc in each st around. (6 sc) Move marker each round.

ROUND 3 [Sc in next st, inc in next st] around. (9 sc)

ROUND 4 Sc in each st around. (9 sc)

ROUND 5 [Sc in each of next 2 sts, inc in next st] around. (12 sc)

ROUND 6 Sc in each st around. (12 sc)

ROUND 7 [Sc in each of next 3 sts, inc in next st] around. (15 sc)

ROUND 8 Sc in each st around. (15 sc)

ROUND 9 [Sc in each of next 4 sts, inc in next st] around. (18 sc)

ROUND 10 Sc in each st around. (18 sc)

ROUND 11 [Sc in each of next 5 sts, inc in next st] around. (21 sc)

ROUND 12 Sc in each st around. (21 sc)

ROUND 13 [Sc in each of next 6 sts, inc in next st] around. (24 sc)

ROUND 14 Sc in each st around. (24 sc)

ROUND 15 [Sc in each of next 7 sts, inc in next st] around. (27 sc)

ROUND 16 Sc in each st around. (27 sc) Sl st in next st to finish off, leaving a long tail for sewing.

CROCODILE ASSEMBLY – Use photo as guide

Attach Body to Head - Position Neck on base of Head. Using long tail and yarn needle, sew in place, stuffing the Neck firmly before finishing off.

Attach Arms - Lift the Collar and using long tails and yarn needle, sew Arms to either side of the Body at Round 41.

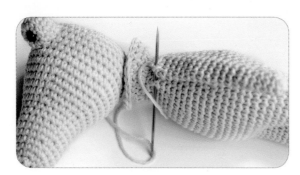

Sewing Arms to Body

Tail – Position Tail at back of Body and using long tail and yarn needle, sew in place.

Position of Tail

Nostrils – Using a long strand of MC, embroider about 5-6 small stitches on either side of Round 1 of Head to create nostrils.

Embroidering Nostrils

Buttons – Position the buttons on front of sweater and sew in place.

Sewing on buttons

Nutmeg the Squirrel

NUTMEG IS NOT YOUR AVERAGE SQUIRREL, HE IS VERY SHY AND HARD TO SPOT AMONGST THE TREE'S IN THE PARK. HE LOVES TO EAT LOTS OF COLOURED BERRIES AND HIS TAIL HAS TURNED STRIPY BECAUSE OF THIS

finished size

About 9½" (24 cm) tall.

materials

» **DMC Natura Just Cotton**
  » **Main Color (MC)** Agatha (#44) – 1½ oz (50 g); 170 yd (155 m)
  » **Tail Colors** - small amounts of each
    » **Color A** Myosotis (#102)
    » **Color B** Light Green (#12)
    » **Color C** - Rose Layette (#06) (and for Cheeks)
    » **Color D** Bleu Layette (#05)

» Size C-2 (2.75 mm) Crochet Hook - or size suitable for yarn used. (Main Hook)

» Dark Grey Embroidery Floss (or Yarn) – for Eyes
» Black Embroidery Floss (or Yarn) – for Nose
» Toy Stuffing

HEAD

ROUND 1 (Right Side) Starting at top of Head, using MC, make a Magic Ring *(see Techniques)*; ch 1, 6 sc in ring; DO NOT JOIN. (6 sc) Tug tail to tighten ring. Mark last stitch.

ROUND 2 [2 sc in next st] around. (12 sc) Move marker each round.

ROUND 3 [Sc in next st, inc *(see Special Stitches)* in next st] around. (18 sc)

ROUND 4 [Sc in each of next 2 sts, inc in next st] around. (24 sc)

ROUND 5 [Sc in each of next 3 sts, inc in next st] around. (30 sc)

ROUND 6 [Sc in each of next 4 sts, inc in next st] around. (36 sc)

ROUND 7 [Sc in each of next 5 sts, inc in next st] around. (42 sc)

ROUND 8 [Sc in each of next 6 sts, inc in next st] around. (48 sc)

ROUNDS 9-14 Sc in each st around. (54 sc)

ROUND 15 Sc in each of next 11 sts, [inc in next st] 3 times, sc in each of next 20 sts, [inc in next st] 3 times, sc in each of next 11 sts. (54 sc)

ROUND 16 Sc in each st around. (48 sc)

ROUND 17 Sc in each of next 13 sts, [inc in next st] 3 times, sc in each of next 22 sts, [inc in next st] 3 times, sc in each of next 13 sts. (60 sc)

ROUNDS 18-21 Sc in each st around. (60 sc)

ROUND 22 [Sc in each of next 8 sts, sc-dec *(see Special Stitches)*] around. (54 sc)

ROUND 23 [Sc in each of next 7 sts, sc-dec] around. (48 sc)

ROUND 24 [Sc in each of next 6 sts, sc-dec] around. (42 sc)

ROUND 25 [Sc in each of next 5 sts, sc-dec] around. (36 sc)

ROUND 26 [Sc in each of next 4 sts, sc-dec] around. (30 sc)

Start stuffing Head firmly (making sure to shape the cheek pouches), adding more as you go.

ROUND 27 [Sc in each of next 3 sts, sc-dec] around. (24 sc)

ROUND 28 [Sc in each of next 2 sts, sc-dec] around. (18 sc)

ROUND 29 [Sc in next st, sc-dec] around. (12 sc)

ROUND 30 [Sc-dec] around. (6 sc) Finish stuffing the Head. Fasten off and close *(see Techniques)*.

EARS (Make 2)

ROW 1 (Right Side) Starting with a long tail (for sewing Ears to Head), make a Magic Ring, 6 sc in ring. DO NOT JOIN.

After Row 1 – 6 sc in ring.

ROWS 2-3 Ch 1, turn, sc in each st across. (6 sc)

After Row 3.

ROW 4 Ch 1, turn, sc-dec, sc in each of next 2 sts, sc-dec (4 sc)

ROW 5 Ch 1, turn, sc in each st across. (4 sc)

ROW 6 Ch 1, turn, sc in first st, sc-dec, sc in last st. (3 sc)

ROW 7 Ch 1, turn, sc in each st across. (3 sc)

ROW 8 Ch 1, turn, sc-dec, sc in last st. (2 sc)

ROW 9 Ch 1, turn, sc in each st across. (2 sc) Finish off and weave in tail.

After Row 9 – the finished Ear.

HEAD ASSEMBLY – Use photos as guide

Ears – Tug tail to close Magic Ring and secure. Holding the Head with stuffed cheek pouches on either side, position and sew the Ears to either side at the top of the Head, at about Round 5.

Eyes - Using the Floss, embroider Sleepy Eyes (see Embroidery Stitches) between Round 16 & 17, with about 7 stitches between them.

LEGS (Make 2)

ROUND 1 (Right Side) Using MC, make a Magic Ring; ch 1, 6 sc in ring; DO NOT JOIN. (6 sc) Tug tail to tighten ring. Mark last stitch.

ROUND 2 [2 sc in next st] around. (12 sc) Move marker each round.

ROUND 3 [Sc in next st, inc in next st] around. (18 sc)

ROUNDS 4-10 Sc in each st around. (18 sc)

At the end of the Round 10 - for the First Leg, finish off. For the Second Leg, DO NOT FINISH OFF.

BODY

ROUND 11 (Joining Legs) Ch 3, working on First Leg, sc in last st made, sc in each of next 17 sts; working in ch-sts, sc in each of next 3 ch; working on Second Leg, sc in each of next 18 sts, working in unused lps on other side of ch, sc in each of next 3 ch. (42 sc) Move marker to last st made.

ROUNDS 12-30 Sc in each st around. (42 sc)

ROUND 31 [Sc in each of next 5 sts, sc-dec] around. (36 sc)

ROUNDS 32-33 Sc in each st around. (36 sc)

Start stuffing Legs and Body firmly, adding more as you go.

ROUND 34 [Sc in each of next 4 sts, sc-dec] around. (30 sc)

ROUNDS 35-36 Sc in each st around. (30 sc)

ROUND 37 [Sc in each of next 3 sts, sc-dec] around. (24 sc)

ROUNDS 38-39 Sc in each st around. (24 sc)

At the end of Round 39, sl st in next st to finish off, leaving a long tail for sewing.

ARMS (Make 2)

ROUND 1 (Right Side) Using MC, make a Magic Ring; ch 1, 8 sc in ring; DO NOT JOIN. (8 sc) Tug tail to tighten ring. Mark last stitch.

ROUNDS 2-18 Sc in each st around. (8 sc) Move marker each round.

LAST ROW Flatten the last round and working through both thicknesses, sc in each of next 4 sc. Finish off leaving a long tail for sewing.

TAIL

ROUND 1 (Right Side) Starting at tip of Tail, using Color A, make a Magic Ring; ch 1, 6 sc in ring; DO NOT JOIN. (6 sc) Tug tail to tighten ring. Mark last stitch.

ROUND 2 Sc in each st around. (6 sc) Move marker each round.

ROUND 3 [Sc in next st, inc in next st] around, changing to Color B in last st. (9 sc)

ROUND 4 With Color B, sc in each st around. (9 sc)

ROUND 5 [Sc in each of next 2 sts, inc in next st] around. (12 sc)

ROUND 6 Sc in each st around, changing to Color C in last st. (12 sc)

ROUND 7 With Color C, [sc in each of next 3 sts, inc in next st] around. (15 sc)

ROUND 8 Sc in each st around. (15 sc)

ROUND 9 [Sc in each of next 4 sts, inc in next st] around, changing to Color D in last st. (18 sc)

ROUND 10 With Color D, sc in each st around. (18 sc)

ROUND 11 [Sc in each of next 5 sts, inc in next st] around. (21 sc)

ROUND 12 Sc in each st around, changing to Color A in last st. (21 sc)

ROUND 13 With Color A, [sc in each of next 6 sts, inc in next st] around. (24 sc)

ROUND 14-15 Sc in each st around. (24 sc)

At the end of Round 15, change to Color B in last st.

ROUNDS 16-18 With Color B, sc in each st around. (24 sc)

At the end of Round 18, change to Color C in last st.

ROUNDS 19-21 With Color C, sc in each st around. (24 sc)

At the end of Round 21, change to Color D in last st.

ROUND 22 With Color D, sc in each st around. (24 sc)

ROUND 23 [Sc in each of next 2 sts, sc-dec] around. (18 sc)

ROUND 24 [Sc in next st, sc-dec] around, changing to MC in last st. (12 sc)

Stuff the Tail firmly. Do not stuff the remaining rounds.

ROUNDS 25-30 Sc in each st around. (12 sc)

LAST ROW Flatten the last round and working through both thicknesses, sc in each of next 6 sc. Finish off leaving a long tail for sewing.

Last Row of Tail - working through both thicknesses.

CHEEKS (Make 2) ·····································

ROUND 1 (Right Side) Using Color C, make a Magic Ring; ch 1, 6 sc in ring; join with sl st to first sc. Finish off leaving a long tail for sewing.

SQUIRREL ASSEMBLY – Use photo as guide ······················

Attach Body to Head - Position Neck on Round 27 of Head. Using long tail and yarn needle, sew in place, stuffing the Neck firmly before finishing off.

Attaching Body to Head.

Arms - Using long tails and yarn needle, sew Arms to either side of the Body at Round 37.

Tail – Position Tail at back of Body and using long tail and yarn needle, sew in place (photo #1). Insert needle back into Body, bringing it out about 10 rounds up (photo #2) and then through a few stitches on Tail (photo #3). Insert needle back into Body bring out at base. Make a double knot to secure and hide tail inside Body.

Photo #1

Photo #2

Photo #3

Cheeks – Position Cheeks on either side of Head. Using long tails and yarn needle, sew in place.

Nose – Using Floss, embroider a Nose, 2 rounds below the Eyes.

Chest Stitches – Using the Tail Colors, embroider a row of V-stitches across the front of the Body, each row a different color, in the same color order of the Tail.

Embroidering V-stitches.

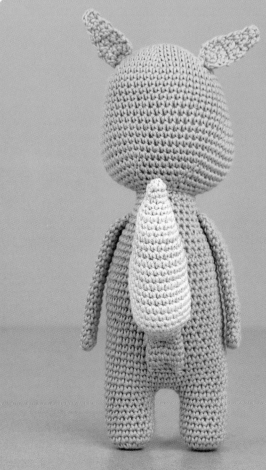

Lucy Lamb

LUCY IS ALWAYS MAKING HER FRIENDS GIGGLE, SHE HAS A VERY CONTAGIOUS LAUGH AND YOU CAN'T HELP BUT SMILE WHEN SHE IS AROUND. SHE LOVES TO DANCE AND HER FAVOURITE FOOD IS CHINESE TAKE-AWAY

finished size

About 10½" (27 cm) tall.

materials

- » **DMC Woolly 5**
  - » **Main Color (MC)** Natural (#03) –3½ oz (100 g); 174 yd (160 m)
  - » **Color A** Mustard (#103) – 1 oz (28 g); 50 yd (45 m) for Hooves

- » **DMC Natura Yummy Cotton**
  - » **Color B** Sichuan (N99) – small amount for Scarf

- » **DMC Natura Just Cotton**
  - » **Color C** Glicine (#30) – small amount for Scarf

- » Size E-4 (3.50 mm) Crochet Hook - or size suitable for yarn used. (Main Hook)
- » Size D-3 (3.25 mm) Crochet Hook – for Scarf

- » Black or Dark Grey Embroidery Floss (or Yarn) – for Eyes and Nose
- » Toy Stuffing

- » **Note** Use Main Hook throughout, unless otherwise stated.

PATTERN STITCHES

Modified Half-Double Crochet (m-hdc)

The normal hdc is Yarn over hook, insert hook in stitch or space indicated, yarn over and pull up a loop (3 loops on hook). Yarn over and pull through all loops on hook.

The modified hdc has this difference Yarn over hook, insert hook in stitch or space indicated, yarn under (or hook over) and pull up a loop (3 loops on hook). Yarn over and pull through all loops on hook.

Invisible Decrease in pattern stitch (inv-dec)

Yarn over hook, insert hook in front loop of next stitch and then in front loop of the following stitch (4 loops on hook), yarn under (or hook over) and pull up a loop through the 2 front loops (3 loops on hook). Yarn over and pull through all loops on hook.

HEAD

ROUND 1 (Right Side) Starting at tip of Nose, using MC, make a Magic Ring *(see Techniques)*; ch 1, 6 sc in ring; DO NOT JOIN. (6 sc) Tug tail to tighten ring. Mark last stitch.

ROUND 2 [2 sc in next st] around. (12 sc) Move marker each round.

ROUND 3 Sc in each st around. (12 sc)

ROUND 4 [Sc in next st, inc *(see Special Stitches)* in next st] around. (18 sc)

ROUND 5 Sc in each st around. (18 sc)

ROUND 6 [Sc in each of next 2 sts, inc in next st] around. (24 sc)

ROUND 7 Sc in each st around. (24 sc)

ROUND 8 [Sc in each of next 3 sts, inc in next st] around. (30 sc)

ROUND 9 Sc in each st around. (30 sc)

ROUND 10 [Sc in each of next 4 sts, inc in next st] around. (36 sc)

ROUNDS 11-15 M-hdc *(see Pattern Stitches)* in each st around. (36 sts)

ROUND 16 [M-hdc in each of next 4 sts, inv-dec *(see Special Stitches)*] around. (30 sts)

Start stuffing Head firmly, adding more as you go.

ROUND 17 [M-hdc in each of next 3 sts, inv-dec] around. (24 sts)

ROUND 18 [M-hdc in each of next 2 sts, inv-dec] around. (18 sts)

ROUND 19 [M-hdc in next st, inv-dec] around. (12 sts)

ROUND 20 [Inv-dec] around. (6 sts) Finish stuffing the Head. Fasten off and close *(see Techniques)*.

EARS (Make 2)

ROUND 1 (Right Side) Starting at tip of Ear, using MC, make a Magic Ring; ch 1, 6 sc in ring; DO NOT JOIN. (6 sc) Tug tail to tighten ring. Mark last stitch.

ROUND 2 [2 sc in next st] around. (12 sc) Move marker each round.

ROUND 3 Sc in each st around. (12 sc)

ROUND 4 [Sc in next 2 st, inc in next st] around. (18 sc)

ROUNDS 5-7 Sc in each st around. (18 sc)

ROUND 8 [Sc in next st, sc-dec *(see Special Stitches)*] around. (12 sc)

ROUNDS 9-12 Sc in each st around. (12 sc)

At the end of Round 12, sl st in next st to finish off, leaving a long tail for sewing.

HEAD ASSEMBLY – Use photos as guide

Ears – Using long tails and yarn needle, position Ears on either side of Head at Round 15 of Head, and sew in place.

Eyes - Using floss, embroider Eyes and Nose.

LEGS (Make 2)

ROUND 1 (Right Side) Using Color A, make a Magic Ring; ch 1, 6 sc in ring; DO NOT JOIN. (6 sc) Tug tail to tighten ring. Mark last stitch.

ROUND 2 [2 sc in next st] around. (12 sc) Move marker each round.

ROUND 3 [Sc in next st, inc in next st] around. (18 sc)

ROUND 4 [Sc in each of next 2 sts, inc in next st] around. (24 sc)

ROUNDS 5-6 Sc in each st around. (24 sc)

ROUND 7 [Sc in each of next 2 sts, sc-dec] around. (18 sc)

ROUND 8 Sc in each st around, changing to MC in last st. (18 sc)

ROUNDS 9-16 With MC, sc in each st around. (18 sc)

At the end of the Round 16 - for the First Leg, finish off. For the Second Leg, DO NOT FINISH OFF.

BODY

ROUND 17 (Joining Legs) Ch 3, working on First Leg, sc in last st made, sc in each of next 17 sts; working in ch-sts, sc in each of next 3 ch; working on Second Leg, sc in each of next 18 sts, working in unused lps on other side of ch, sc in each of next 3 ch. (42 sc) Move marker to last st made.

ROUNDS 18-20 Sc in each st around. (42 sc)

ROUNDS 21-25 M-hdc in each st around. (42 sts)

ROUND 26 [M-hdc in each of next 5 sts, inv-dec] around. (36 sts)

ROUND 27 M-hdc in each st around. (36 sts)

ROUND 28 [M-hdc in each of next 4 sts, inv-dec] around. (30 sts)

Start stuffing Legs and Body lightly, adding more as you go. (Note Take care not to over-stuff and stretch out the stitches.)

ROUND 29 M-hdc in each st around. (30 sts)

ROUND 30 [M-hdc in each of next 3 sts, inv-dec] around. (24 sts)

ROUND 31 M-hdc in each st around. (24 sts)

ROUND 32 [M-hdc in each of next 2 sts, inv-dec] around. (18 sts)

ROUND 33-34 M-hdc in each st around. (18 sts)

At the end of Round 34, sl st in next st to finish off, leaving a long tail for sewing.

ARMS (Make 2)

ROUND 1 (Right Side) Using Color A, make a Magic Ring; ch 1, 6 sc in ring; DO NOT JOIN. (6 sc) Tug tail to tighten ring. Mark last stitch.

ROUND 2 [2 sc in next st] around. (12 sc) Move marker each round.

ROUNDS 3-5 Sc in each st around. (12 sc)

ROUND 6 [Sc in next st, sc-dec] around, changing to MC in last st. (8 sc)

ROUNDS 7-18 With MC, sc in each st around. (8 sc)

Stuff Hand firmly and stuff Arm lightly.

LAST ROW Flatten the last round and working through both thicknesses, sc in each of next 4 sc. Finish off leaving a long tail for sewing.

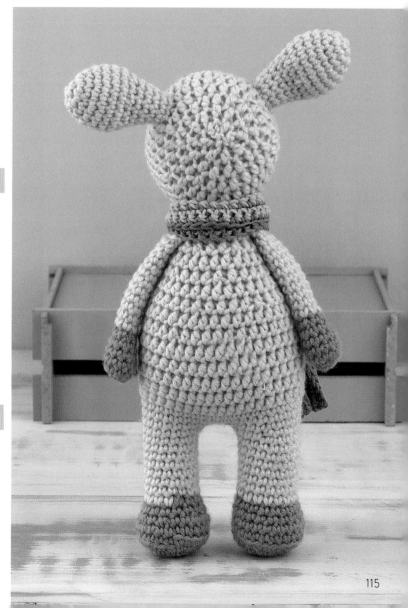

SCARF

ROW 1 Using Color B and smaller hook, ch 101; sc in 2nd ch from hook, [sc in next ch] across, changing to Color C in last st. (100 sc)

ROW 2 With Color C, sc in each st across, changing to Color B in last st. (100 sc)

ROW 3 With Color C, sc in each st across, changing to Color C in last st. (100 sc)

ROW 4 Repeat Row 2. Do not change color. Finish off and weave in all ends.

LAMB ASSEMBLY – Use Photo As Guide

Body – Finish stuffing Body and position at base of Head. Using long tail and yarn needle, sew in place, stuffing the neck before closing.

Arms – Using long tails and yarn needle, position the Arms on either side of the Body at about Round 33, and sew in place.

Scarf – Wrap Scarf around neck.

Lack Whale and Poppy Narwhal

MILO'S DAYS ARE SPENT ON THE SEA-SHORE WATCHING THE SHIPS SAIL BY. HE DREAMS OF ONE DAY BECOMING A SEA-CAPTAIN OF HIS OWN BOAT

finished size

About 4" (10 cm) tall and 6" (15 cm) long.

materials

» **DMC Natura Just Cotton**
  » **For Whale**
    » **Main Color** Bleu Layette (#05) – 1½ oz (50 g); 170 yd (155 m)

  » **For Narwhal**
    » **Main Color** Rose Layette (#06) – 1½ oz (50 g); 170 yd (155 m)
      Small amounts of various colors for Flowers and Leaves.

  » **For Both**
    » **Color A** Ibiza (#01) – small amounts for Horn (Nawhal) & Water Spout (Whale)

» Size D-3 (3.25 mm) Crochet Hook - or size suitable for yarn used. (Main Hook)

» 1$\frac{1}{32}$" (9 mm) Safety Eyes – 2 per toy

» Toy Stuffing

» **Notes**

1. Two strands of yarn are held together throughout. Either use two separate balls of same color, or use the center pull and outer pull of same ball.

2. Use Main Hook throughout, unless otherwise stated.

ROUND 1 (Right Side) Starting at bottom of belly, holding 2 strands of Main Color together, make a Magic Ring *(see Techniques)*; ch 1, 6 sc in ring; DO NOT JOIN. (6 sc) Tug tail to tighten ring. Mark last stitch.

ROUND 2 [2 sc in next st] around. (12 sc) Move marker each round.

ROUND 3 [Sc in next st, inc *(see Special Stitches)* in next st] around. (18 sc)

ROUND 4 [Sc in each of next 2 sts, inc in next st] around. (24 sc)

ROUND 5 [Sc in each of next 3 sts, inc in next st] around. (30 sc)

ROUND 6 [Sc in each of next 4 sts, inc in next st] around. (36 sc)

ROUND 7 [Sc in each of next 5 sts, inc in next st] around. (42 sc)

ROUND 8 [Sc in each of next 6 sts, inc in next st] around. (48 sc)

ROUND 9 (Tail) Ch 11, 2 sc in 2nd ch from hook, sc in each of next 9 ch, sc in same st as last sc worked on Round 8 *(see photo)*, sc in each of next 48 sc; working in unused lps on other side of starting ch, sc in each of next 9 ch, 2 sc in last ch. (71 sc) Mark last sc made. Move marker each round.

Round 9 - Working in the last sc worked on Round 8.

ROUND 10 Inc in next st, sc in each st around, inc in last st. (73 sc)

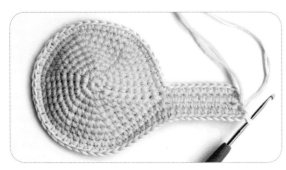

Working the Tail rounds.

ROUND 11 Sc in each st around. (73 sc)

ROUND 12 [Sc-dec *(see Special Stitches)*] twice, sc in each of next 65 sts, [sc-dec] twice. (69 sc)

ROUND 13 [Sc-dec] twice, sc in each of next 61 sts, [sc-dec] twice. (65 sc)

Working the Tail decreases.

ROUND 14 [Sc-dec] twice, sc in each of next 57 sts, [sc-dec] twice. (61 sc)

ROUND 15 [Sc-dec] twice, sc in each of next 53 sts, [sc-dec] twice. (57 sc)

ROUND 16 [Sc-dec] twice, sc in each of next 49 sts, [sc-dec] twice. (53 sc)

ROUND 17 [Sc-dec] twice, sc in each of next 45 sts, [sc-dec] twice. (49 sc)

Finished Tail tip.

ROUND 18 Sc-dec, sc in each of next 47 sts. (48 sc)

ROUNDS 19-26 Sc in each st around. (48 sc)

With the Tail at the back, insert Safety Eyes on either side of face at front, between Rounds 16 & 17, about 13-14 stitches apart.

Position of Eyes.

ROUND 27 [Sc in each of next 6 sts, sc-dec] around. (42 sc)

ROUND 28 [Sc in each of next 5 sts, sc-dec] around. (36 sc)

Start stuffing toy firmly, adding more as you go.

ROUND 29 [Sc in each of next 4 sts, sc-dec] around. (30 sc)

ROUND 30 [Sc in each of next 3 sts, sc-dec] around. (24 sc)

ROUND 31 [Sc in each of next 2 sts, sc-dec] around. (18 sc)

ROUND 32 [Sc in next st, sc-dec] around. (12 sc)

ROUND 33 [Sc-dec] around. (6 sc) Finish stuffing the toy. Fasten off and close (see Techniques), leaving a long tail for sewing Eyelids.

HORN (for Narwhal Only)

ROUND 1 (Right Side) Holding 2 strands of Color A together, make a Magic Ring; ch 1, 4 sc in ring; DO NOT JOIN. (4 sc) Tug tail to tighten ring.

ROUND 2 Sc in each st around. (4 sc) Mark last sc and move marker each round.

ROUND 3 [Sc in next st, inc in next st] around. (6 sc)

ROUND 4 Sc in each st around. (6 sc)

ROUND 5 [Sc in next st, inc in next st] around. (9 sc)

ROUNDS 6-7 Sc in each st around. (9 sc)

ROUND 8 [Sc in next st, inc in next st] 4 times, sc in last st. (13 sc)

ROUNDS 9-12 Sc in each st around. (13 sc)

At the end of Round 12, sl st in next st to finish off, leaving a long tail for sewing.

TAIL FINS (Make 2)

ROUND 1 (Right Side) Holding 2 strands of Main Color together, make a Magic Ring; ch 1, 6 sc in ring; DO NOT JOIN. (6 sc) Tug tail to tighten ring. Mark last stitch.

ROUND 2 [2 sc in next st] around. (12 sc) Move marker each round.

ROUNDS 3-5 Sc in each st around. (12 sc)

ROUND 6 [Sc in next st, sc-dec] around. (8 sc)

ROUND 7 Sc in each st around. (8 sc) Sl st in next st to finish off, leaving a long tail.

CHEEKS (Make 2)

ROUND 1 (Right Side) Using Color C, make a Magic Ring; ch 1, 8 sc in ring; join with sl st to first sc. (8 sc) Finish off leaving a long tail for sewing.

FLORAL CROWN (for Narwhal Only)

Note Refer to the photos of the Flowers and Leaves in Rhiannon the Bunny.

Flowers (Make 3 in different colors)

ROUND 1 (Right Side) Make a Magic Ring; [ch 6, sl st in ring] 5 times. Tug tail to tighten ring. Finish off leaving a long tail for sewing.

Leaf (Make 3 using different greens)

ROUND 1 (Right Side) Make a Magic Ring; ch 1, (sc, hdc, dc, picot (see Special Stitches) dc, hdc, sc) in ring; DO NOT JOIN. Tug tail to tighten ring. Finish off leaving a long tail for sewing.

TOY ASSEMBLY – Use photos as guide

Eyelids – Using long tail and yarn needle, insert needle from closure, through head, bringing it out above one Eye. Embroider 3 stitches over the top of the eye to create an eyelid. Repeat for other Eye. Secure and finish off.

Horn (for Narwhal) – Stuff the Horn tightly, using the end of your hook to reach the point of the Horn. Position the Horn about 4 rounds down from top of Head and using long tail and yarn needle, sew in place.

Embroidering Eyelids.

Position of Horn and attaching Fins to Tail tip.

Tail Fins – Flatten each Fin. Using long tails and yarn needle, sew Fins to tip of Tail.

Cheeks – Position Cheeks on either side of Head. Using long tails and yarn needle, sew in place.

Water Spout (for Whale only) – Holding a few short strands of Color A together, fold in half. Insert hook under a stitch at the top of the head and place the fold on hook.

Pull strands halfway through to form a loop. Pull the tails of strands through the loop and pull tightly to knot. Trim the ends to desired length. Separate the yarn strands and fan them out.

Floral Crown (for Narwhal only) – Sew a Leaf to each Flower. Position Flowers and Leaves around Horn and sew in place.

Milo the Monkey

MILO'S DAYS ARE SPENT ON THE SEA-SHORE WATCHING
THE SHIPS SAIL BY. HE DREAMS OF ONE DAY BECOMING A
SEA-CAPTAIN OF HIS OWN BOAT

finished size

About 15" (38 cm) tall – including Hat.

materials

» **DMC Woolly 5**
  » **Main Color (MC)** Pale Blue (#71) – 3½ oz (100 g); 272 yd (250 m)
  » **Color A** Natural (#03) – small amounts for Muzzle & Inner Ears

» **DMC Natura Just Cotton**
  » **Color B** Ibiza (#01) – small amounts for T-Shirt & Hat
  » **Color C** Blue Night (#53) – small amount for T-Shirt & Hat Embroidery

» Size E-4 (3.50 mm) Crochet Hook - or size suitable for yarn used. (Main Hook)

» Size D-3 (3.25 mm) Crochet Hook – for T-Shirt & Hat

» $^{11}/_{32}$" (9 mm) Safety Eyes – 2

» Brown Embroidery Floss (or Yarn) – for Nose

» Toy Stuffing

Note Use Main Hook throughout, unless otherwise stated.

HEAD

ROUND 1 (Right Side) Starting at the tip of Muzzle, using Color A, make a Magic Ring *(see Techniques)*; ch 1, 6 sc in ring; DO NOT JOIN. (6 sc) Tug tail to tighten ring. Mark last stitch.

ROUND 2 [2 sc in next st] around. (12 sc) Move marker each round.

ROUND 3 [Sc in next st, inc *(see Special Stitches)* in next st] around. (18 sc)

ROUND 4 [Sc in each of next 2 sts, inc in next st] around. (24 sc)

ROUND 5 [Sc in each of next 3 sts, inc in next st] around. (30 sc)

ROUND 6 [Sc in each of next 4 sts, inc in next st] around. (36 sc)

ROUNDS 7-8 Sc in each st around. (36 sc)

At the end of Round 8, change to MC in last st.

ROUND 9 Sc in each of next 15 sts, [inc in next st] 6 times, sc in each of next 15 sts. (42 sc)

ROUND 10 Sc in each of next 18 sts, [inc in next st] 6 times, sc in each of next 18 sts. (48 sc)

ROUND 11 Sc in each st around. (48 sc)

ROUND 12 [Sc in each of next 7 sts, inc in next st] around. (54 sc)

ROUNDS 13-19 Sc in each st around. (54 sc)

Showing Face Shaping.

Insert Safety Eyes on either side of face shaping, between Rounds 10 & 11, about 18 stitches apart.

Placement of Safety Eyes.

ROUND 20 [Sc in each of next 7 sts, sc-dec *(see Special Stitches)*] around. (48 sc)

ROUND 21 [Sc in each of next 6 sts, sc-dec] around. (42 sc)

ROUND 22 [Sc in each of next 5 sts, sc-dec] around. (36 sc)

Start stuffing Head firmly, adding more as you go.

ROUND 23 [Sc in each of next 4 sts, sc-dec] around. (30 sc)

ROUND 24 [Sc in each of next 3 sts, sc-dec] around. (24 sc)

ROUND 25 [Sc in each of next 2 sts, sc-dec] around. (18 sc)

ROUND 26 [Sc in next st, sc-dec] around. (12 sc)

ROUND 27 [Sc-dec] around. (6 sc) Finish stuffing the Head. Fasten off and close *(see Techniques)*, leaving a long tail for sewing Eyelids.

EARS

Inner Ear (Make 2)

ROUNDS 1-3 (Right Side) Using Color A and smaller hook, repeat Round 1 to 3 of Head.

At the end of Round 3, there are 18 sc. Sl st in next st to finish off and weave in ends.

Outer Ear (Make 2)

ROUNDS 1-5 (Right Side) Using MC and Main Hook, repeat Rounds 1 to 3 of Inner Ear, but DO NOT FINISH OFF. (18 sc)

Ear Assembly Holding an Inner and Outer Ear with wrong sides together, with Outer Ear facing, working through both thicknesses using back loops of Outer Ear and front loops of Inner Ear, matching stitches, sc in each st around. (18 sc)

Sl st in next st to finish off, leaving a long tail for sewing. Repeat for other Ear.

Joining Outer and Inner Ear

HEAD ASSEMBLY – Use photos as guide

Eyelids – Using Tail from Head and yarn needle, insert needle from closure, through Head, bringing it out above one Eye. Embroider 2-3 Straight Stitches *(see Embroidery Stitches)* over the top of the eye to create an eyelid. Insert needle back through Head and repeat for other Eye. Insert needle through Head and bring out at base (where it will be attached to Body). Secure and finish off.

Embroidering Eyelids above Eyes.

Nose - Using the Floss, embroider Nose. Make a few horizontal stitches, and one straight vertical stitch.

Embroidering the Nose

Ears – Position and sew the Ears to either side at the top of the Head in line with the Eyes, at about Round 18.

Attached Ears.

BODY

ROUNDS 1-6 Using MC, repeat Rounds 1 to 6 of Head.

At the end of Round 6, there are 36 sc.

ROUND 7 [Sc in each of next 5 sts, inc in next st] around. (42 sc)

ROUNDS 8-16 Sc in each st around. (42 sc)

ROUND 17 [Sc in each of next 5 sts, sc-dec] around. (36 sc)

ROUNDS 18-19 Sc in each st around. (36 sc)

Start stuffing Body firmly, adding more as you go.

ROUND 20 [Sc in each of next 4 sts, sc-dec] around. (30 sc)

ROUNDS 21-22 Sc in each st around. (30 sc)

ROUND 23 [Sc in each of next 3 sts, sc-dec] around. (24 sc)

ROUNDS 24-25 Sc in each st around. (24 sc)

ROUND 26 [Sc in each of next 2 sts, sc-dec] around. (18 sc)

ROUNDS 27-28 Sc in each st around. (18 sc)

At the end of Round 28, sl st in next st to finish off, leaving a long tail for sewing.

ARMS (Make 2)

ROUND 1 (Right Side) Using MC, make a Magic Ring; ch 1, 6 sc in ring; DO NOT JOIN. (6 sc) Tug tail to tighten ring. Mark last stitch.

ROUND 2 [2 sc in next st] around. (12 sc) Move marker each round.

ROUND 3 [Sc in next st, inc in next st] around. (18 sc)

ROUNDS 4-8 Sc in each st around. (18 sc)

ROUND 9 [Sc in each of next 4 sts, sc-dec] around. (15 sc)

ROUNDS 10-11 Sc in each st around. (15 sc)

ROUND 12 [Sc in each of next 3 sts, sc-dec] around. (12 sc)

ROUNDS 13-14 Sc in each st around. (12 sc)

Stuff the Hand lightly.

ROUND 15 [Sc in each of next 2 sts, sc-dec] around. (9 sc)

LEGS (Make 2)

ROUNDS 1-20 Using MC, repeat Rounds 1 to 20 of Arms.

Stuff the Feet lightly.

ROUNDS 21-28 Sc in each st around. (9 sc)

LAST ROW Flatten the last round and working through both thicknesses, sc across to close. Finish off leaving a long tail for sewing.

T-SHIRT

ROUND 1 (Right Side) Using Color B and smaller hook, ch 50; taking care not to twist chain, join with sl st to first ch to form a ring; ch 1, sc in same ch as joining, [sc in next ch] around. DO NOT JOIN. (50 sc) Mark last stitch.

ROUND 2 Sc in each st around, changing to Color C in last st. (50 sc) Move marker each round.

After 2 rounds, changing colors.

ROUNDS 3-4 With Color C, sc in each st around. (50 sc)

At the end of Round 4, change to Color B in last st.

ROUNDS 5-6 With Color B, sc in each st around. (50 sc)

At the end of Round 6, change to Color C in last st.

ROUNDS 7-10 Repeat Rounds 3 to 6.

ROUNDS 11-12 Repeat Rounds 3 to 4.

ROUND 13 With Color B, [sc in each of next 8 sts, sc-dec] around. (45 sc)

ROUND 14 Sc in each st around, changing to Color C in last st. (45 sc)

ROUNDS 16-20 Sc in each st around. (9 sc)

LAST ROW Flatten the last round and working through both thicknesses, sc across to close. Finish off leaving a long tail for sewing.

TAIL

ROUND 1 (Right Side) Using MC, make a Magic Ring; ch 1, 8 sc in ring; DO NOT JOIN. (8 sc) Tug tail to tighten ring. Mark last stitch.

ROUNDS 2-30 Sc in each st around. (8 sc) Move marker each round.

At the end of Round 30, sl st in next st to finish off, leaving a long tail for sewing.

After 14 rounds, before Armholes.

ROUND 15 (Armholes) With Color C, sc in each of next 8 sts, ch 10, skip next 8 sc, sc in each of next 13 sts, ch 10, skip next 8 sc, sc in each of next 8 sts. (29 sc & 2 ch-10 lps)

ROUND 16 Sc-dec, sc in each of next 6 sts, sc in each of next 10 ch, sc in each of next 13 sts, sc in each of next 10 ch, sc in each of next 6 sts, sc-dec, changing to Color B in last st. (47 sc)

ROUND 17 With Color B, sc-dec, sc in each of next 43 sts, sc-dec. (45 sc)

ROUND 18 Sc in each st around. (45 sc) Sl st in next st to finish off. Weave in all ends.

COLLAR

ROW 1 Turn the shirt upside down and with Color B and smaller hook, join with sl st to the 12th st to the right of center front st (photo #1), ch 1, sc in same st as joining, sc in each of next 2 sts, hdc in each of next 3 sts, dc in each of next 3 sts, tr in each of next 3 sts, ch 4, sl st in same st as last tr, sl st in next 2 sts (photo #2), ch 4, tr in same st as last sl st, tr in each of next 2 sts, dc in each of next 3 sts, hdc in each of next 3 sts, sc in each of next 3 sts, sl st in next st to finish off (photo #3). Weave in all ends.

Photo #2

Photo #3

Photo #1

MONKEY ASSEMBLY – Use photo as guide ···

Body – Finish stuffing Body and position at base of Head. Using long tail and yarn needle, sew in place, stuffing the neck firmly before closing.

Arms – Using long tails and yarn needle, position the Arms on either side of the Body at about Round 27, and sew in place.

Legs – Position the Legs at the front of the Body on Round 6, with one stitch between them. Using long tails and yarn needle, sew in place.

Tail – Position the Tail at the back of the Monkey on Round 8, and sew in place.

T-Shirt - Pull the T-Shirt up over the Legs onto the Body and slip the Arms into the armholes.

Hat – Using Color C, embroider an anchor to the front of Hat. Sew the Hat, at an angle, on the Monkey's head.

Embroidering an anchor on the Brim.

HAT

ROUNDS 1-6 Using Color B and smaller hook, repeat Rounds 1-6 of Head.
At the end of Round 6, there are 36 sc.

ROUNDS 7-14 Sc in each st around. (36 sc)
At the end of Round 14, sl st in next st to finish off. Weave in ends.

Hat Brim

ROUND 1 Turn Hat upside down, working in BLO *(see Techniques)* on last round, join Color B with sl st to any st, ch 1, [sc in next st] around. DO NOT JOIN. (36 sc) Mark last stitch.

ROUND 2 Working in both loops, sc in each of next 8 sts, inc in next st, sc in each of next 17 sts, inc in next st, sc in each of next 8 sts. (38 sc)

ROUNDS 3-6 Sc in each st around. (38 sc)

At the end of Round 6, sl st in next st to finish off. Weave in all ends.

Working in BLO on first round of Brim.